BABY NAMES

A COMPREHENSIVE GUIDE TO CHOOSING A NAME (INCLUDING 3000+ BABY NAMES WITH MEANING AND ORIGIN)

Disclaimer

While all attempts have been made to verify the information provided in this publication, neither the author nor the publisher assumes any responsibility for errors, omissions or contrary interpretations of the subject matter herein.

This book is for entertainment purposes only. The views expressed are those of the author alone, and should not be taken as expert instruction or commands. The reader is responsible for his or her own actions.

Adherence to all applicable laws and regulations, including international, federal,

CONTENTS

INTRODUCTION

Welcome dear `soon to be parent´. Congratulations, I'm very excited for you and your family. Before we start, let me just commend you first; you've made a great decision in purchasing this book. That decision means that you care about your baby. And that's one quality that great parents have. Within this book, you'll receive tons of ideas as well as a few tips and crucial mistakes to avoid when choosing a name.

Selecting a name for your baby can be overwhelming. It's likely that your friends and family will start offering you suggestions - whether or not you asked for it. I know the feeling.

Now unlike other books, this is not a book that is about lecturing you or giving you my opinions. This is a book that contains facts, and its primary purpose is to give you ideas -

not opinions. However, that does not mean that you will go without guidance throughout this book. But I've tried to keep the "advice giving" to a minimum. I'm confident that you'll appreciate that once you start reading this book.

Thank you very much for choosing this book. I will do my best to offer you as much value as possible in regards to the topic of baby names.

PART 1:

How to Choose A Name For Your Baby

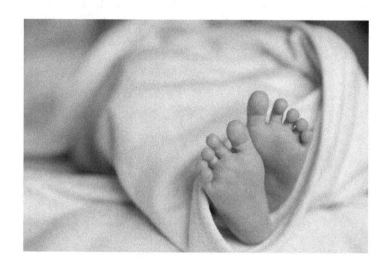

Chapter 1 – How to Successfully Choose a name for your baby

The purpose of this book is not to advise you in regards to picking a name. I know that you're most likely looking for ideas and perhaps a tiny bit of guidance. I know, however, that the process of choosing a name can be very overwhelming. Therefore, I've decided to at least make 10-20% of the book about tips and guidance. If you feel that these tips are obvious, feel free to go directly to the names. But for some of you, I think you'll appreciate these two chapters. Please understand that there's no right or wrong way to go about picking a name. But to make it less overwhelming for you, I've created a step by step process to successfully choosing a name for your baby.

Step 1: Look for Inspiration

How great! You've already started the process by opening this book. You'll find a lot of names here that will serve as inspiration for you.

STEP 2: SAY THE NAME OUT LOUD
In this step, I recommend that you think critically about the name that you've chosen. Take it through a verbal test. For example, go over potential mispronunciations or any unwanted attention that the name can bring to your child. If it passes this test, it's time to move onto step number 3.

STEP 3: LOOK OVER THESE THINGS
In this step, it's time to look at a few more things before you approve the name. Here they are in no order of importance:

- **Initials.** Can the initials lead to an uncomfortable nickname in school?
- **Look for the meaning.** A lot of names have a meaning attached to them. I've done extensive research for you and created this book that contains a lot of meanings. Take advantage of that and if – contrary to expectation – you wouldn't find

the right name here, just research the meaning on your own by using Google.

- **Think about the future.** Your child will not be young forever. Therefore, think about names that will do well when he or she is an adult as well. For example, Binky or Bunny might be cute names when the child is a baby. But what about when your kid reaches the age of 40?

CHAPTER 2 – CRUCIAL MISTAKES TO AVOID

We've already gone over the importance of checking the initials as well as looking at potential mispronunciations. In this chapter, I will give you a few more tips and things to think about. I will do this by giving you mistakes that other parents have done when choosing a name. Hopefully, this will allow you to avoid these pitfalls.

- **Not thinking about potential nicknames.** This is a colossal mistake that can cause your child a lot of suffering in school. Therefore, always make sure to go over the nicknames together with your last name as well.
- **Choosing a name that is too complicated.** This mistake can cause your child to endure a lifetime of corrections. "Excuse me, my name is actually…"

- **Overpopularity.** Some people might not view this as an actual mistake. And it isn't, as long as the person is aware of the fact that the name is very popular. For example, if a famous star is choosing this name for his or her baby – expect that it will rise in popularity.
- **They don't think about email handles.** Be honest, have you thought about this? It's definitely not the first thing that one thinks about. It might even be hard to imagine that one day, your baby will have its own email handle attached to a school or job. So for example, if your child's name is Ajani Erkson. And they join a school that has a system that generates email addresses based on initials (first two letters and first three letters). The child might end up with the email address being: ajerk@harvard.com
- **Not searching for the name on Google.** It's always wise to search for the name on Google before you've chosen it. What if the name

is a bad name to live up to? For example, it might be the same as a bunch of criminals or other types of people. A simple Google search will allow you to avoid this mistake.

- **Not looking over the meaning.** For example, the name Marie means "a sea of bitterness." So not all names have positive meanings attached to it. Therefore, always make it a habit to look up the meaning of the name.

PART 2:

GIRL NAMES THAT MEANS SOMETHING

CHAPTER 3 – GIRL BABY NAMES THAT MEAN BEAUTIFUL

Please do not misinterpret the title of part 2. There are a lot more names than these that contains meaning. Therefore, don't feel discouraged if you can't find the perfect name here. I have 3000 more for you in part 3 that also contains meaning. But these names are sorted by a specific word – in this case: beautiful.

- Anwen, Origin: Welsh
- Kunani, Origin: Hawaiian
- Hermosa, Origin: Spanish
- Anahi, Origin: Persian, Spanish
- Navit, Origin: Hebrew
- Jaffa, Origin: Hebrew
- Annabella, Origin: Latin, English
- Zaina, Origin: Arabic

- Vashti, Origin: Persian
- Rupali, Origin: Indian
- Lulabelle, Origin: American
- Kelis, Origin: American
- Ella, Origin: Spanish, English, Greek
- Eavan, Origin: Celtic, Gaelic
- Shayna, Origin: Yiddish, Hebrew
- Belle, Origin: French
- Calista, Origin: Greek
- Callalily, Origin: Greek
- Kimi, Origin: Japanese
- Maribel, Origin: Spanish, Mexican, French
- Sohna, Origin: Indian
- Miki, Origin: Japanese
- Trixibelle, Origin: American
- Beila, Origin: French, Spanish
- Bellamy, Origin: French
- Nefertiti, Origin: Egyptian, Ancient Egyptian
- Shifra, Origin: Hebrew
- Calliope, Origin: Greek
- Zaniah, Origin: Arabic
- Aloha, Origin: Hawaiian
- Belva, Origin: Latin
- Olathe, Origin: Native American
- Yamilla, Origin: Arabic

- Mieko, Origin: Japanese
- Belinda, Origin: Latin, Spanish
- Jamilla, Origin: Arabic
- Clarabell, Origin: Latin
- Yaffa, Origin: Hebrew
- Kalidas, Origin: Greek
- Gamila, Origin: Arabic
- Kennis, Origin: Gaelic
- Calla, Origin: Greek
- Hiraani, Origin: Hawaiian
- Ilona, Origin: Greek, Hungarian
- Arabella, Origin: English, Latin
- Ella, Origin: English
- Teagan, Origin: Celtic, Irish, Welsh
- Rosabelle, Origin: French, Italian
- Farrah, Origin: English
- Mirabella, Origin: Latin
- Christabel, Origin: English, Latin
- Bella, Origin: Hebrew, Latin
- Mika, Origin: Japanese
- Alika, Origin: Swahili

CHAPTER 4 – GIRL BABY NAMES THAT MEAN ANGEL

- Tangi, Origin: American
- Angie, Origin: Greek, Latin
- Angel, Origin: Greek
- Angelica, Origin: Latin, Greek
- Serafina, Origin: Spanish, Hebrew
- Angeline, Origin: French, Latin, Russian
- D'Angela, Origin: American
- Gina, Origin: Greek, Italian
- Angela, Origin: Greek, French, Mexican
- Heaven, Origin: American, English

- Zeraphina, Origin: Hebrew
- Angelique, Origin: French, Greek
- Dangelo, Origin: Italian, Greek
- Angelina, Origin: Greek, Latin
- Seraphim, Origin: Hebrew

CHAPTER 5 – GIRL BABY NAMES THAT MEAN PEACE

- Paz, Origin: Hebrew, Spanish
- Pacifica, Origin: Spanish
- Peace, Origin: English
- Frederica, Origin: Teutonic, German
- Luba, Origin: Polish
- Malu, Origin: Hawaiian
- Chesney, Origin: French, English
- Pax, Origin: Latin
- Frida, Origin: Teutonic, German
- Noah, Origin: Hebrew
- Iraina, Origin: Russian
- Alana, Origin: Celtic, Old German, Irish
- Pace, Origin: English
- Fia, Origin: Italian, Scottish
- Noa, Origin: Hebrew
- Lana, Origin: Celtic, Old German, English
- Frieda, Origin: Teutonic, German
- Irene, Origin: Greek
- Noé, Origin: Hebrew
- Jerusalem, Origin: Hebrew
- Amandeep, Origin: Sanskrit

- Dove, Origin: English
- Naima, Origin: Arabic
- Malia, Origin: Hebrew, Hawaiian
- Shalom, Origin: Hebrew
- Serena, Origin: Latin
- Salomé, Origin: Hebrew
- Yen, Origin: Vietnamese
- Winifred, Origin: Celtic, German
- Shiloh, Origin: Hebrew
- Shanti, Origin: Sanskrit
- Zell, Origin: Hebrew
- Selima, Origin: Hebrew
- Serenity, Origin: English, Latin

CHAPTER 6 – GIRL BABY NAMES THAT MEAN HAPPY

- Beatrice, Origin: Latin
- Desdemona, Origin: Greek
- Radhiya, Origin: African, Swahili
- Felice, Origin: Italian, Latin
- Merry, Origin: English
- Felicia, Origin: Latin
- Ada, Origin: Teutonic, Hebrew, English
- Gaye, Origin: English
- Beatrix, Origin: English, Latin
- Alaia, Origin: Arabic, Basque
- Sharmila, Origin: Hindi, Indian
- Adamaris, Origin: American
- Blythe, Origin: English
- Trixie, Origin: English, Latin
- Keiko, Origin: Japanese
- Bea, Origin: American, English
- Felicity, Origin: Latin, English

CHAPTER 7 – GIRL BABY NAMES THAT MEAN LOVE

- Cheri, Origin: French
- Aphrodite, Origin: Greek
- Amoretta, Origin: Latin
- Gael, Origin: Celtic, English, Greek
- Esmé, Origin: French
- Amy, Origin: French, Portuguese, Latin
- Cher, Origin: French
- Brisa, Origin: Spanish
- Aimee, Origin: French
- Amara, Origin: Greek
- Dodie, Origin: Hebrew
- Filippa, Origin: Greek
- Derica, Origin: Teutonic, German
- Carissa, Origin: French, Greek
- Davida, Origin: Hebrew
- Caris, Origin: Welsh

- Cherish, Origin: English
- Cerie, Origin: Welsh
- Habiba, Origin: Arabic
- Amanda, Origin: Latin
- Ceridwen, Origin: Welsh
- Gertrude, Origin: Teutonic, German
- Halia, Origin: Greek, Hawaiian
- Didi, Origin: Hebrew
- Paris, Origin: Greek, French
- Leba, Origin: Yiddish
- Xylophia, Origin: Greek
- Pandora, Origin: Greek
- Kyla, Origin: Celtic, Scottish, Hebrew
- Suki, Origin: Japanese
- Maite, Origin: Spanish
- Kalila, Origin: Arabic
- Phillipa, Origin: Greek
- Ludmilla, Origin: Russian, Slavic
- Tanith, Origin: African, Phoenician
- Myrna, Origin: Arabic, Celtic, Irish
- Nayeli, Origin: American, Latin, Native American
- Thandie, Origin: African
- Taffy, Origin: Welsh
- Nahid, Origin: Persian
- Yaretzi, Origin: Aztec, American
- Karissa, Origin: Greek

- Venus, Origin: Greek, Latin
- Sherry, Origin: Hebrew, English, French
- Heart, Origin: English
- Lida, Origin: Russian, Slavic
- Laramie, Origin: French
- Pleasant, Origin: English

CHAPTER 8 – GIRL BABY NAMES THAT MEAN PRINCESS

- Sarahi, Origin: Hebrew
- Sarai, Origin: Hebrew
- Soraya, Origin: Persian
- Sari, Origin: Arabic, Hebrew
- Tiana, Origin: Greek, Latin
- Suri, Origin: Persian, Hebrew
- Zara, Origin: Arabic, Hebrew
- Amira, Origin: Arabic, Hebrew
- Zadie, Origin: English
- Sally, Origin: Hebrew, English
- Sariah, Origin: Hebrew
- Sadie, Origin: Hebrew
- Elmira, Origin: Arabic
- Sarita, Origin: Indian, Hebrew
- Zaria, Origin: Russian, Latin, Hebrew
- Sarah, Origin: Hebrew
- Damita, Origin: Spanish
- Tia, Origin: Greek, Spanish

PART 3:

GIRL NAMES THAT MEANS SOMETHING

CHAPTER 9 – BOY BABY NAMES THAT MEAN HANDSOME

- Keane, Origin: English, Celtic
- Beauregard, Origin: French
- Yahir, Origin: American, Arabic
- Shaquille, Origin: African, Arabic
- Bello, Origin: French
- Jamal, Origin: Arabic
- Jamel, Origin: Arabic
- Beau, Origin: French
- Kavan, Origin: Celtic, Irish
- Jamir, Origin: Arabic
- Wasim, Origin: Arabic
- Jamari, Origin: French, Arabic
- Kenneth, Origin: Celtic, Scottish, Irish
- Yamil, Origin: Arabic
- Japheth, Origin: Hebrew
- Cullen, Origin: Celtic, Irish
- Kenna, Origin: Celtic, Scottish, Irish
- Hassan, Origin: Arabic

- Alan, Origin: Celtic, Old German, Irish
- Kevin, Origin: Celtic, Irish
- Jamar, Origin: African, Arabic
- Jamil, Origin: Arabic
- Kavanaugh, Origin: Irish
- Cavan, Origin: Celtic, Irish
- Yaphet, Origin: Hebrew

CHAPTER 10 – BOY BABY NAMES THAT MEAN STRONG

- Valeria, Origin: Italian, Latin
- Boaz, Origin: Hebrew
- Fergus, Origin: Celtic, Irish
- Andrew, Origin: Greek
- Kemen, Origin: Spanish, Basque
- Valerie, Origin: French, Latin
- Quinlan, Origin: Celtic, Irish
- Valentin, Origin: Spanish, Latin
- Willard, Origin: Teutonic, German

- Armstrong, Origin: English
- Brian, Origin: Celtic, Irish, Scottish
- Charles, Origin: Teutonic, Old German, German
- Ekon, Origin: Nigerian
- Valery, Origin: Russian, Latin
- Ezra, Origin: Hebrew
- Djimon, Origin: West African
- Humberto, Origin: Teutonic, Portuguese
- Plato, Origin: Greek
- Durell, Origin: English, French
- Raynor, Origin: English, Scandinavian
- Valentino, Origin: Italian
- Kwan, Origin: Chinese, Korean
- Etai, Origin: Hebrew
- Andreas, Origin: Teutonic, Greek
- Bogart, Origin: Teutonic, French
- Anders, Origin: Greek, Scandinavian
- Gerrit, Origin: Teutonic, Dutch
- Ragnar, Origin: English, Scandinavian
- Emmett, Origin: English, German
- Ethan, Origin: Hebrew
- Richmond, Origin: Teutonic, German

- Quigley, Origin: Celtic, Irish
- Neon, Origin: Greek
- Eberhard, Origin: Teutonic, German
- Ellard, Origin: Teutonic, German
- Barrett, Origin: English, German
- Remo, Origin: English, Greek
- Charlie, Origin: Teutonic, Old German, German
- Andrea, Origin: Greek

CHAPTER 11 – BOY BABY NAMES THAT MEAN MAN

- Romany, Origin: Romany
- Ansel, Origin: French, German
- Pompey, Origin: Latin
- Eugene, Origin: Greek
- Gerard, Origin: Teutonic, English
- Charles, Origin: Teutonic, Old German, German
- Manning, Origin: English
- Gregory, Origin: Greek, Latin
- Richard, Origin: English, Old German
- Bono, Origin: Latin
- Cartman, Origin: English
- Quenby, Origin: Scandinavian
- Mackean, Origin: Scottish
- Patrick, Origin: Latin
- Almanzo, Origin: Old German
- Edgar, Origin: English, Old English
- Marques, Origin: Spanish, Portuguese
- Jermaine, Origin: Latin
- Bwana, Origin: Swahili

- Alexander, Origin: Greek
- Freeman, Origin: English
- Thurgood, Origin: English
- Truman, Origin: English
- Dermot, Origin: Celtic, Irish
- Andreas, Origin: Teutonic, Greek
- Declan, Origin: Celtic, Gaelic, Irish
- Fabrizio, Origin: Italian
- Medgar, Origin: German
- Desmond, Origin: Celtic, Irish, Gaelic
- Garrett, Origin: English, Old German, Irish
- Roger, Origin: English, Old German, German
- Ryder, Origin: English, Old English
- Manley, Origin: English
- Apollo, Origin: Greek
- Karl, Origin: Teutonic, German
- German, Origin: Spanish, French, English
- Gavrie, Origin: Russian
- Marquis, Origin: French
- Jove, Origin: Latin, Greek
- Steadman, Origin: English
- Abraham, Origin: Hebrew
- Manfred, Origin: Teutonic, English
- Francesco, Origin: Latin, Italian

- Rodman, Origin: English, German
- Oscar, Origin: English, Old English, Scandinavian
- Earl, Origin: Celtic, English, Old English
- Macleod, Origin: English, Gaelic
- Gerardo, Origin: Spanish, German
- Whitman, Origin: English
- Wentworth, Origin: English
- Ellsworth, Origin: Hebrew, English
- Flynn, Origin: Celtic, Irish
- Fabrice, Origin: Italian
- Fisher, Origin: English, Old English
- Manny, Origin: Spanish, English
- Quimby, Origin: Scandinavian
- Lenno, Origin: Native American
- Rutger, Origin: Dutch, Scandinavian
- Duke, Origin: English, French
- Jarvis, Origin: English, Old English, German
- Archer, Origin: English
- Anders, Origin: Greek, Scandinavian
- Kale, Origin: Hawaiian
- Armand, Origin: Teutonic, German
- Wayman, Origin: English
- Janus, Origin: Latin
- Andrew, Origin: Greek
- Gatlin, Origin: English

- Howard, Origin: English, Old English
- Yancey, Origin: Native American
- Germaine, Origin: French
- Bolton, Origin: English
- Eugenie, Origin: Greek
- Armando, Origin: Teutonic, German, Spanish
- Adam, Origin: Hebrew
- Jerry, Origin: Greek, English, German
- Paine, Origin: Latin
- Butch, Origin: American
- Carl, Origin: English, Teutonic, Old German, German
- Saxon, Origin: English
- Destry, Origin: French, English
- Foster, Origin: English
- Whit, Origin: English
- Ibrahim, Origin: Arabic, Hebrew
- Gregor, Origin: Greek, Dutch
- Forsythe, Origin: Gaelic
- Manzie, Origin: American

CHAPTER 12 – BOY BABY NAMES THAT MEAN KING

- Rex, Origin: Latin
- Pomeroy, Origin: French
- Prince, Origin: Latin
- Leroy, Origin: French, Portuguese
- Naresh, Origin: Indian, Hindi
- Common, Origin: English
- Basil, Origin: Greek
- Elroy, Origin: French

- Roy, Origin: Celtic, Irish, French
- Kingston, Origin: English
- Rey, Origin: French, Spanish
- Kendrick, Origin: English, Welsh
- Ryan, Origin: Celtic, Irish
- Waverly, Origin: English
- Ray, Origin: French, Old German
- Kingsley, Origin: English
- Obba, Origin: Yoruban
- Reynaldo, Origin: Teutonic, Spanish
- Kenwood, Origin: English
- Pippin, Origin: French, German
- LeBron, Origin: African
- Balthazar, Origin: English, Greek
- Wassili, Origin: Greek
- Melchior, Origin: Arabic
- Reynolds, Origin: Celtic, English
- Ryne, Origin: American, Irish
- Delroy, Origin: French
- Kinsley, Origin: English, Celtic, American
- Eze, Origin: African
- Ara, Origin: Armenian, American, Arabic

PART 4:

3000 BABY NAMES AND TOP LISTS

CHAPTER 13 – 3000 BABY NAMES

Here you'll find 3000 baby names. Most of them contain a meaning as well as an origin. On the left side you'll have the name. On the right side of the name, you'll find the meaning. And to the left, you'll have origin. Enjoy!

- Kacie, vigorous. Origin: English, American
- Jinny, Origin: English
- Thorp, From the village. Origin: English
- Garmond, Spear protector. Origin: English
- Charis, Dear one; darling. Origin: English, Greek
- Gale, Lively. Origin: English, American, Irish
- Kacia, vigorous. Origin: English

- Joan, Gift from God. Origin: Hebrew, American, English, Shakespearean
- Maree, Bitter. Origin: English, French
- Garrson, Son of Gar. Origin: English
- Carolyne, Feminine manly. Origin: English, American
- K.C. meaning: alert, vigorous. Origin: English
- Graden, Gray-haired: son of the Gray family; son of Gregory. Origin: English
- Hunter, Hunter. Origin: English, American
- Rawiella, From the deer spring. Origin: English
- Egbertina, Shining sword. Origin: English
- Jayna, Jehovah has been gracious; has shown favor. Origin: English
- Ashten, Town of ash trees. Origin: English
- Dagwood, Bright wood; from the bright one's forest. Origin: English
- Innocent, Innocent. Origin: English, Latin
- Bronsen, Son of a dark man. Origin: English
- Attewater, From the waterside. Origin: English
- Kacey, Origin: English, American

- Roland, Famous. Origin: Latin, Swedish, Teutonic, American, English, French, German
- Aethelbert Noble or bright. Origin: English, Anglo-Saxon
- Bradyn, From the broad valley. Origin: English, American
- Dereck, Leader. Origin: English, American, German
- Kendra, Prophetess. Origin: Anglo-Saxon, American, English
- Audene, Nobility; strength. Origin: English
- Faegan, Joyful. Origin: English
- Etheldreda, Origin: English
- Cicely, Origin: English
- Oberon, Origin: English, German, Shakespearean
- Marshal, Steward. Also, a law enforcement officer's title. Origin: English, American, French
- Captain, He who is in charge. Origin: English
- Buddy, Friend. Origin: English, American
- Herne, Mythical hunter god. Origin: Celtic, English

- Hadley, Field of heather. Surname. The name of Hemingway's first wife. Origin: English, American
- Norvyn, From the north. Origin: Teutonic, English
- Barr, Bard; travelling musician/singer. Origin: Irish, English
- Neelie, Feminine of Neil, meaning champion. Origin: English, Gaelic
- Jaclyn, Origin: English, American
- Dana, Wise. Intelligent. Origin: Muslim, American, Norse, Scandinavian, English, Hebrew
- Clayborne, From the clay brook. Origin: English
- Lion, Lion. Origin: English, Shakespearean
- Mindy, Love. Origin: German, American, English
- Kaia, The sea. Origin: Hawaiian, American, Greek
- Birdine, Little bird. Origin: English
- Huntingdon, From the hunter's hill. Origin: English
- Fulton, From the people's estate. Origin: English
- Danette, God has judged. Origin: Hebrew, American, English, French

- Bradig, From the broad island. Origin: English
- Charley, man. Origin: English, American
- Brindley, Burnt wood. Origin: English
- Garnet, Origin: English, French, American
- Edgar, Fortunate and powerful. Origin: English, American, Anglo-Saxon, Shakespearean
- Nedda, Feminine of Ned. Origin: English
- Bardon, Minstrel; a singer-poet. Origin: Celtic, English
- Slaton, From the valley farm. Origin: English
- Jeremy, in use since the Middle Ages. Origin: English, American, Hebrew
- Sherry, darling or dear one. Origin: English, American
- Hollis, The holly tree. Common name given Christmas girl babies. Origin: English
- Kandyce, Modern- ancient hereditary title used by Ethiopian queens. Origin: English
- Burhdon, Lives at the castle. Origin: English
- Chatwyn, Warring friend. Origin: English

- Atmore, From the moor. Origin: English
- Deon, God. Origin: African-American, American, English, French
- Origin: English, Irish, French, Berkeley, From the birch meadow. Origin: Anglo-Saxon, Irish, English, Shakespearean
- Carolus, Strong. Origin: French, Gaelic, English
- Sabrina, Legendary princess. Origin: English, American, Italian, Latin
- Kaila, The laurel crown. Origin: Israeli, American, English, Hawaiian
- Aescby, From the ash tree farm. Origin: English
- Rich, Wealthy. Origin: English, American, German
- Cleve, Cliffs. Abbreviation of Cleveland. Origin: English, American
- Daviel, Beloved. Origin: English
- Fauna, Fawn. Origin: French, Latin, English
- Thomkins, Little Tom. Origin: English
- Beachy, Close to beech trees. Origin: English
- Jaynie, Jehovah has been gracious; has shown favor. Origin: English, Hebrew

- Olney, From Olney. Origin: English
- Alberteen, noble. Origin: English
- Fairlay, Bull meadow. Origin: English
- Mel, Meaning uncertain. Origin: English, American
- Phelps, Son of Philip. Origin: English
- Brodrig, From the broad ridge. Origin: English
- Belden, Lives in the beautiful glen. Origin: English, Teutonic
- Humphrey, Supports Peace. Origin: Teutonic, American, German, English, Shakespearean
- Graeham, From the gray home. Origin: English
- Boote, House. Origin: English
- Betsey, Origin: English
- Burnie, Small river or stream with an island. Origin: English
- Jena, Origin: English, American
- Melbourne, From the mill stream. Origin: English
- Hagley, From the hedged enclosure. Origin: English
- Livia, Olive. Origin: Latin, English
- Cameo, A carved gem portrait. Origin: English, Italian

- Neal, Origin: English, American, Celtic, Irish
- Fabion, Origin: English, Latin
- Lintun, From the flax enclosure. Origin: English
- Bentley, From the meadow. Origin: English
- Norwood, From the north forest. Origin: English, American
- Dexter, From a surname meaning 'dyer'. Origin: English, American, Latin
- Odwolfe, Wealthy wolf. Origin: English
- Alger, Noble spearman. Origin: Anglo-Saxon, German, English, Teutonic
- Bardalph, Ax wolf. Origin: English
- Cim, Ruler. Origin: English
- Holden, Gracious. Origin: Teutonic, American, English
- Brick, Bridge. Origin: English
- Diamanda, Of high value; brilliant. Origin: English
- Becca, Abbreviation of Rebecca. Origin: English
- Huntingden, From the hunter's hill. Origin: English
- Chelsa, a London district. Origin: English
- Berthold, Bright light. Origin: English, German

- Brooklyn, Water; stream. Origin: English, American
- Hagly, From the hedged enclosure. Origin: English
- Kandee, Modern- ancient hereditary title used by Ethiopian queens. Origin: English
- Grafere, Lives in the grove. Origin: English
- Christophoros, Christ bearer. Origin: Greek, English
- Laciann, Origin: English, French
- Marchland, From the march. Origin: English
- Lisha, sweet; honest. Origin: English, American
- Dereka, Gifted ruler. Modern feminine of Derek. Origin: English
- Attkins, Son of Aiken. Origin: English
- Bronson, Son of a dark man. Origin: English, American, Anglo-Saxon, German
- Law, From the hill. Origin: English
- Barden, Minstrel; a singer-poet. Origin: Celtic, English

- Richard, Powerful ruler. Origin: Teutonic, American, English, Shakespearean, French, German
- Cherilynn, Rhyming. Origin: English
- Charlton, A, meaning peasants' settlement. Origin: English
- Meldon, From the hillside mill. Origin: English
- Aleta, Winged. Origin: English, Latin, Spanish, American, Greek
- Caldwiella, From the cold spring. Origin: English
- Denlie, Meadow by a valley. Origin: English
- Chance, Good luck; good fortune; chancellor. Origin: English, American, French
- Mady, Maiden. Origin: English, German
- Bailee, Courtyard within castle walls. Origin: English, French, American
- Kendyl, Royal valley, referring to Kent in England. Origin: English
- Aisley, Dwells at the ash tree meadow.Origin: Anglo-Saxon, English
- Geordie, Farmer. Origin: Greek, English
- Pernel, Little rock. Origin: English

- Laurenne, place of honor and victory. Origin: English, Latin
- Eddie, Prosperous protector. Origin: French, American, English
- Bernard, Strong as a bear. See also Bjorn. Origin: English, American, German
- Avalee, given names Avis and Aveline. Origin: English
- Ayrwode, From the fir forest. Origin: English
- Tedmund, Wealthy defender. Origin: Anglo-Saxon, Teutonic, English
- Berry, A name derived from the fruit. Origin: English
- Irwyn, Sea lover. Origin: Anglo-Saxon, English
- Bridgeley, From the meadow near the bridge. Origin: English
- Brette, Brit. A native of England: (Britain). Origin: English, French
- Lawe, From the hill. Origin: English
- Albreda, Origin: English
- Beric, Grain farm. Origin: English
- Beverly, From the beaver meadow. Origin: English, American

- Guy, warrior. Origin: Teutonic, American, Latin, Hebrew, French, Celtic, English, German
- Bay, auburn-haired. Origin: English, French, Vietnamese
- Bryanne, Strong. She ascends. Feminine of Brian. Origin: Celtic, English
- Melinda, Gentle. Origin: Greek, American, Latin, English
- Branda, beverage brandy used as a given name. Origin: English
- Adrion From Adria: (Adriatic sea region.) Origin: English, Latin
- Bel, White. Origin: Czechoslovakian, English, French, German, Latin, Spanish
- Garrad, from Gerald 'rules by the spear. Origin: English
- Brenten, Hilltop. Origin: Celtic, English
- Caersewiella, Lives at the watercress spring. Origin: English
- Christie, Christian. Origin: Scottish, English
- Mabel, Beautiful, loving. Origin: Latin, American, English
- Aiekin, Oaken. Origin: English
- Birkit, Area of birch trees. Origin: English

- Kathy, Pure. Origin: Greek, American, French, Latin, Irish, English
- Beechy, Close to beech trees. Origin: English
- Joanie, Origin: English
- Carmine, Garden. Origin: English, American, Hebrew
- Salhford, From the willow ford. Origin: English
- Bronsson, Son of a dark man. Origin: English
- Estcott, From the east cottage. Origin: English
- Chetwyn, From the cottage on the winding path. Origin: English
- Salena, Moon goddess. Origin: Greek, English, Latin
- Oleta, Winged. Origin: English, American
- Balder, Prince. Origin: Scandinavian, English, Norse
- Vayle, Lives in the valley. Origin: English, French
- Brock, Origin: German, American, English
- Kadian, Rhyming, meaning pure. Origin: English

- Biford, Lives at the river crossing. Origin: English
- Daley, Lives in the valley. Origin: English, Irish
- Aethelind, An Old English name from an Old German name meaning noble snake. Origin: English
- Aldis, From the old house. Origin: English
- Chick, a man. Origin: English
- Jonni, Modern feminine of John and Jon. Origin: English
- Frazier, French town. Origin: English, American, Scottish
- Dontay, Contemporary phonetic'enduring. Origin: English
- Audris, Nobility; strength. Origin: English
- Albina, From the Latin Albinus, meaning white. Origin: Latin, American, English
- Chadburne, From the wildcat brook. Origin: English
- Alexandrina, Alexander meaning defender of man Origin: English, Greek
- Ashlinn, Meadow of ash trees. Origin: English
- Kenelm, Defends the family. Origin: English

- Came, Joy. Origin: English
- Genaya, White wave. Origin: English
- Attheaeldre, At the elder tree. Origin: English
- Cerelia, Mistress; lady. Feminine of Cyril. Origin: English, Italian, Latin
- Kacee, vigorous. Origin: English
- Jen, Fair and yielding. Origin: Cornish, English, Scottish
- Beorhthram, Bright raven. Origin: English
- Dericka, Gifted ruler. Modern feminine of Derek. Origin: English
- Dael, Lives in the valley. Origin: English
- Leoline, Leader. Lion-like. Origin: English, Welsh
- Beresford, From the barley ford. Origin: English
- Shepherd, Shepherd. Origin: English, Shakespearean
- Baron, Noble fighter. Origin: Teutonic, American, English, French, Hebrew
- Zinnia, Flower name. Origin: English
- Ashleigh, Meadow of ash trees. Origin: English, American
- Attlee, From the meadow. Origin: English

- Fairlie, From the bull's pasture. Origin: English
- Vern, Origin: English, French, American
- Jollene, Origin: English
- Bliss, Happy. Origin: Anglo-Saxon, English
- Salina, Moon goddess. Origin: Greek, American, English, Latin
- Jaylynn, Feminine. Origin: English, American
- Skylor, Phonetic spelling of Schuyler. Origin: English
- Audelia, Nobility; strength. Origin: English
- Talmadge, Tall. Origin: English, American
- Odam, Son in law. Origin: English
- Dewey, Cherished; Beloved. Origin: Hebrew, American, Welsh, English
- Ackerley, Dweller at the acre meadow. Origin: English
- Bliss, Happy. Origin: Anglo-Saxon, English
- Bentlee, From the meadow. Origin: English
- Barnard, Strong as a bear. Origin: German, English
- Cary, From the fortress. Origin: Celtic, American, English, Irish, Welsh

- Nancy, Grace. Origin: Hebrew, American, French, English
- Brydger, Lives at tbe bridge. Origin: English
- Mildred, Mild of strength. Origin: English, American, Anglo-Saxon
- Baylee, Steward; bailiff. Origin: English
- Beeman, Beekeeper. Origin: English
- Calli, Lark. Origin: English, Greek, Gaelic, Irish
- Hurlbart, Army strong. Origin: English
- Bailee, Steward; bailiff. Origin: English
- Elwell, From the old spring. Origin: English
- Berwynne, Harvest-time friend. Origin: English
- Aethelreda, Noble maiden. Origin: English
- Burdon, Lives at the castle. Origin: English
- Alburn, Noble warrior. Origin: English
- Baubie, foreign or strange, Origin: English
- Blakely, From the light meadow; from the dark meadow. Origin: English, Scandinavian

- Dalwyn, Friend; good friend. Origin: English
- Dorion, Place name in Greece. Origin: Greek, English
- Blaney, Origin: English, Scottish
- Brandyn, Beacon on the hill' or 'gorse-covered hill. Origin: English, American
- Bryant, Strong. Origin: Celtic, American, English, French
- Barrie, Fair-haired. Origin: English, American, French, Irish
- Jimi, Modern feminine of Jimmy. Origin: English
- Garret, Spear strength. Origin: Teutonic, American, English, Irish
- Aldercy, Chief. Origin: English
- Joann, Origin: English, Latin, American
- Parke, Of the forest. Origin: English
- Denman, Resident of a valley. Origin: English
- Ember, Origin: English
- Palmere, Pilgrim. Origin: English
- Fawne, Young deer. Origin: English
- Cherise, dear one; darling. Origin: English, French
- Skyler, Phonetic spelling of Schuyler. Origin: English, American

- Bramwell, From the bramble bush spring. Origin: English
- Slade, From the valley. Origin: English
- Aswyn, Friend with a spear. Origin: English
- Raed, Red. Origin: English
- Buckey, Male deer. Origin: English, Greek
- Yale, From the slope land. Origin: English, Welsh
- Wadanhyll, From the advancer's hill. Origin: English
- Garmund, Spear protector. Origin: English
- Elly, Light. Origin: Irish, English
- Rexford, chieftain; ruler.' Surname. Origin: English, Latin, American
- Rickard, Powerful ruler. Origin: German, English
- Chaunce, Fortune; a gamble. Origin: French, English
- Burneig, Lives on the brook island. Origin: English
- Charlynn, Manly. Origin: English
- Carilynne, Feminine manly. Origin: English
- Brittni, Origin: English, American

- Bardolph, Bright wolf, ax-wielding wolf. Origin: English, German, Shakespearean
- Roisin, Rose (flower name). Origin: English, German
- Aler, From the alder tree. Origin: English
- Ulrica, Universal ruler. Origin: Teutonic, German, English
- Bourke, Lives in a fortress. Origin: French, English
- Eadric, Wealthy ruler. Origin: English
- Brinley, Burnt wood. Origin: English
- Bab, From the gateway. Origin: Arabic, English
- Allred, Wise or red haired man. Origin: English
- Elberta, Intelligent. Origin: Teutonic, American, English
- Audrea, Nobility; strength. Origin: English
- Fawn, Young deer. Origin: English, American
- Milton, From the mill farm. Origin: English, American
- Jeneen, Origin: English
- Baudier, Prince. Origin: Scandinavian, English

- Brandy, The beverage brandy used as a given name. Origin: English, American
- Addney, Lives on the noble's island. Origin: English
- Booth, Herald. Origin: Norse, English, Teutonic
- Bardoul, Bright wolf, ax-wielding wolf. Origin: English
- Aesoburne, Lives near the ash tree brook. Origin: English
- Paine, Pagan. Origin: English, Latin
- Braemwiella, From the bramble bush spring. Origin: English
- Ranell, Strong counselor. Origin: English, Scandinavian
- Briony, The name of a flowering vine used in folk medicine. Origin: Greek, English
- Rickward, Strong guardian. Origin: English
- Charlie, man. Origin: English, American
- Caius, Joy. Origin: Welsh, English, Shakespearean
- Ackley, Dwells at the oak tree meadow. Origin: English
- Verity, Truth. Origin: English

- Peregrine, Origin: English
- Garnell, Keeper of grain. Surname. Origin: English, French
- Osbert, Divinely brilliant. Origin: English
- Bryggere, Lives at tbe bridge. Origin: English
- Carmina, Song. Origin: English, Spanish
- Blaise, Stutters. Origin: English, American, Latin, Arthurian Legend, French
- Chetwin, From the cottage on the winding path. Origin: English
- Denten, Valley town. Origin: English
- Gracie, Grace. Origin: English, American, Irish, Latin
- Candice, Sparkling. Origin: Greek, American, Hebrew, Latin, English
- Perekin, Little rock. Origin: English
- Fred, meaning elf counsel. Origin: English, American, Teutonic, German
- Basilios, Royal; kingly. Origin: English
- Favian, Origin: English, Latin
- Nikkie, Abbreviation of Nicole, meaning victory. Origin: English
- Deeanna, meaning divine. Origin: English
- Daina, From Denmark. Origin: English
- Beore, Birch tree. Origin: English

- Carolina, Song of happiness. Origin: French, American, English, Italian, Latin
- Ashby, From the ash tree farm. Origin: English, Scandinavian
- Ayers, Heir to a fortune. Origin: English
- Blackburn, Black brook. Origin: English
- Baylee, Courtyard within castle walls. Origin: English, French, American
- Zakari, Origin: English
- Chadd, Protector; defender. Origin: English, American
- Aida, Wealthy. Origin: English, American, French, Spanish, Italian
- Aethelbeorn, Noble warrior. Origin: English
- Carree, manly. Origin: English
- Millard, Strong. Origin: French, American, English
- Cindy, Dimunitive of Cynthia, Lucinda, and Cinderella. Origin: English, American
- Opal, Jewel. Origin: Sanskrit, American, English
- Ellia, Abbreviation of Eleanor and Ellen. Origin: English
- Bondig, Free. Origin: English

- Marschall, Steward. Origin: English
- Birkhed, Lives at the birch headland. Origin: English
- Rick, Hard ruler. Origin: German, American, Norse, English
- Madra, Mother. Origin: English
- Ricker, Strong army. Origin: English
- Ashwyn, Spear friend. Origin: English
- Rolando, Famous. Origin: Teutonic, American, French, German, English
- Beorht, Glorious. Origin: English
- Emeline, Hard working. Origin: Teutonic, American, English, French
- Meldryk, From the powerful mill. Origin: English
- Faryn, Adventurous. Origin: English
- Bran, Raven. Origin: Celtic, Gaelic, Welsh, Arthurian Legend, English
- Ellison, Son of Elder. Origin: English
- Burkett, Area of birch trees. Origin: English, French
- Laurelle, bay tree symbolic of honor and victory. Origin: English
- Eadgyth, Wife of Edward the Confessor. Origin: Anglo-Saxon, English
- Cherilyn, Rhyming. Origin: English
- Bellamey, Good-looking companion. Origin: English

- Bailie, Steward; bailiff. Origin: English
- Atleigh, From the meadow. Origin: English
- Camella, flower name Camelia. Origin: English, Latin
- Cis, Origin: English
- Chas, man. Origin: English, American
- Cathia, pure. Origin: English
- Brandyn, beverage brandy used as a given name. Origin: English
- Janai, God has answered. Origin: English
- Jenae, 'God has answered. '. Origin: English
- Ceaster, Lives at the camp. Origin: English
- Audra, Nobility; strength. Origin: French, American, English
- Humility, Humble. Origin: English
- Frazer, French town. Origin: English, Scottish
- Auriar, Gentle music. Origin: English
- Thormund, Thor's protection. Origin: English
- Zavrina, Form of Sabrina: a princess. Origin: English
- Halliwell, Lives by the holy spring. Origin: English

- Ivar, Archer. Origin: Scandinavian, Swedish, Teutonic, English
- Georgia, Farmer. Origin: Greek, American, English, German
- Blaine, Slender. Origin: Celtic, American, Gaelic, English, Scottish, Irish
- Alec, Origin: English, American, Greek, Scottish
- Hadrian, Dark. Origin: Swedish, English, Latin
- Briggere, Lives at tbe bridge. Origin: English
- Chauncy, Chancellor; secretary; fortune; a gamble. Origin: English, French
- Brianna, Strong. Origin: Irish, American, Celtic, English
- Calvert, Cowherd; cowboy. Origin: Englishm
- Hagaward, Keeper of the hedged enclosure. Origin: English
- Birkie, Birch island. Origin: English
- Clemen, Gentle. Origin: English
- Geary, Flexible. Origin: English, American
- Elwyn, meaning noble friend. Origin: English, American, Welsh
- Geraldina, Capable with a spear. Origin: Teutonic, English, German

- Devron, English county name Devon. Origin: English
- Oletha, Light; nimble. Origin: English
- Austen, Origin: English
- Braleah, From the hillslope meadow. Origin: English
- Broderik, From the broad ridge. Origin: English
- Fars, Son of Farr. Origin: English
- Aubree, Rules with elf-wisdom. Origin: English, French, American
- Cecilio, Blind. Origin: Italian, English
- Mabelle, Lovable. Origin: English, American, Latin, French
- Dallton, Dale town; valley town. Origin: English
- Egerton, From the town on the ridge. Origin: English
- Laurence, Origin: Latin, American, English, Shakespearean
- Alhhard, Brave. Origin: English
- Claec, Dark. Origin: English
- Talford, Tall. Origin: English
- Maryan, meaning bitter, Origin: English
- Cedra, Modern feminine of Cedric. Origin: English
- Davison, David's son. Origin: English

- Dace, Of the nobility. Origin: English, French, Gaelic
- Lissa, Bee. Origin: Greek, English
- Aurear, Gentle music. Origin: English
- Bertin, Industrious. Origin: English, Teutonic, Spanish
- Marilyn, Blend of Marie or Mary and Lyn. Origin: English, American, Hebrew
- Alexandria, Defender of man. Origin: Latin, American, English, Greek
- Christen, Christian. Origin: Greek, American, English, Latin
- Radbyrne, Lives by the red stream. Origin: English
- Marwin, Mariner. Origin: Teutonic, English
- Christoph, Christ bearer. Origin: Greek, English
- Allie, A 13th centurymeaning nobility. Now particularly popular in Scotland. Origin: French, American, English, Arabic
- Janais, God has answered. Origin: English
- Bertolde, Bright light. Origin: English, German
- Butch, Butcher. Origin: English, American

- Aldwyn, Defender. Origin: Anglo-Saxon, English
- Clementius, Merciful. Origin: Dutch, English
- Jayna, Jehovah has been gracious; has shown favor. Origin: English
- Katlin, Medieval English form of the Irish Caitlin. Pure. Origin: English, American
- Ashla, Meadow of ash trees. Origin: English
- Clem, Gentle. Origin: English, American, Latin
- Casey, Brave. Origin: Celtic, Gaelic, American, English, Irish
- Marvyn, Famous friend. Origin: English, Celtic, Welsh
- Pfeostun, From the Priest's farm. Origin: English
- Frayn, Foreign. Origin: English
- Audie, Old friend. Origin: English, American
- Hilary, Happy. Origin: Latin, American, English
- Lach, Lives near water. Origin: English
- Yeoman, Retainer. Origin: English
- Lache, Lives near water. Origin: English

- Verena, Protector. Origin: German, English, Teutonic
- Rodwell, Lives by the spring near the road. Origin: English
- Jazlynn, Modern; combination of Jocelyn and the musical term jazz. Origin: English
- Caryn, Modern. Origin: English, American, Latin
- Zak, Origin: English, Hebrew
- Clarey, Clear. Origin: English
- Jenalyn, Origin: English
- Quintrell, Origin: English, French
- Maddie, Woman from Magdala. Origin: English, French
- Lisabet, Devoted to God. Origin: Hebrew, English
- Blakelie, From the light meadow; from the dark meadow. Origin: English
- Favio, Origin: English, Latin
- Oona, One. Origin: English, Latin, Irish
- Nancy, Grace. Origin: Hebrew, American, French, English
- Charlene, Feminine of Charles meaning manly. Origin: French, American, English
- Marsden, From the marsh valley. Origin: English

- Deorwine, Friend of the deer. Origin: English
- Cheryll dear one, darling. Origin: English, American
- Benjie, Right-hand son. Origin: English
- Birkett, Lives at the birch headland. Origin: English
- Bartholomeo, Son of a farmer. Origin: English
- Valentine, Strong. Origin: English, American, Latin, Shakespearean
- Denney, Follower of Dionysius (Greek god of wine). Origin: Greek, English
- Adron From Adria: (Adriatic sea region). Origin: English, Latin
- Boda, Herald. Origin: English
- Hagaleah, From the hedged meadow. Origin: English
- Cindel, Abbreviation of Cynthia and Lucinda. Origin: English
- Christian, Follower of Christ. Origin: English, American, Irish, Greek, Latin
- Brandan, Sword. Origin: Celtic, American, English, Irish

- Ida, A nymph. Origin: Latin, American, English, German, Greek, Irish, Teutonic
- Chaise, Hunter. Origin: English
- Calbert, Cowherd; cowboy. Origin: English
- Athmarr, Noble or famous. Origin: English
- Caine, Place name unrelated to the Biblical Cain. Origin: English, French
- Athelward, Noble protector. Origin: English
- Dorien, Place name in Greece. Origin: Greek, English
- Bentleigh, From the bent grass meadow. Origin: English
- Averell, Wild boar. Origin: English
- Avah, given names Avis and Aveline. Origin: English
- Brocleigh, From the badger meadow. Origin: English
- Bromleah, From the broom covered meadow. Origin: English
- Baiardo, Brown hair. Origin: English
- Dalton, From the farm in the dale. Origin: English, American
- Aescleah, Lives in the ash tree grove. Origin: English

- Doogie, Dark water. Origin: English
- Carleton, Peasants' settlement. Origin: English, American
- Franklin, Free. Origin: Teutonic, American, English
- Estcot, From the east cottage. Origin: English
- Ransom, Son of Rand. Origin: English, American
- Rodney, Famous. Origin: Teutonic, American, English
- Ashlynn, Meadow of ash trees. Origin: English, American
- Birde, Bird. Origin: English
- Garmann, Speannan. Origin: English
- Galena, Festive party. Origin: English, Spanish
- Hamlet, House or home. Introduced from Germany during the Norman Conquest. Also used as a surname. Origin: English, German, Shakespearean
- Addison, Son of Adam. Origin: English, American
- Denny, King Henry the Eighth' Sir Anthony Denny. Origin:

Shakespearean, American, Norse, Greek, English

- Alford, From the old ford. Origin: English, American
- Bruns, Dark of skin. Origin: English
- Clayburn, From the clay brook. Origin: English
- Cecile, 'blind'. Origin: English, American, French, Latin
- Bartle, Ploughman. Son of Talmai. Origin: Hebrew, English
- Berton, Shining friend. Origin: Teutonic, American, English, Spanish
- Katlyn, Medieval English form of the Irish Caitlin. Pure. Origin: English, American
- Claudia, Lame. Origin: Biblical, Latin, Spanish, American, English, German, French
- Lauren, Laurel. Origin: French, American, Latin, English
- Bemeere, Trumpeter. Origin: English
- Brandice, beverage brandy used as a given name. Origin: English
- Valen, Strong. Origin: English, Latin
- Attleigh, From the meadow. Origin: English
- Kala, Black. Origin: Hindi, American

- Osmin, Godly protection. Origin: English, Scandinavian
- Skylar, Phonetic spelling of Schuyler. Origin: English, American
- Vannes, Grain fans. Origin: English
- Aesclin, Lives at the ash tree pool. Origin: English
- Nicson, Son of Nick. Origin: English
- Casimir, Peaceful. Origin: Slavic, American, English, Polish
- Melborn, From the mill stream. Origin: English
- Odwulf, Wealthy wolf. Origin: English
- Doro, Greek Dorothy meaning Gift of God. Origin: English
- Wada, Advancer. Origin: English
- Danrelle, Hidden. Origin: English
- India, The country India. Origin: English, American, Biblical
- Edelina, noble. Origin: Teutonic, German, English
- Ascott, Lives at the east cottage. Origin: English
- Cindia, Abbreviation of Cynthia and Lucinda. Origin: English
- Farun, English surname. Origin: English

- Chet, Camp of the soldiers. Origin: English, American
- Udall, From the yew tree valley. Origin: English
- Bardolf, Axe-wielding wolf. Origin: English
- Christos, follower of Christ; the annointed. Origin: Greek, English
- Favian, Origin: English, Latin
- Jonn, gracious; has shown favor. Origin: English, French
- Chelsey, Place name; a London district. Origin: English, American
- Oakley, From the oak - tree meadow. Origin: English, American
- Lew, Lion. Origin: Latin, Slavic, American, Welsh, English
- Clarance, Clear. Origin: English, American
- Gerald, Spear strength. Origin: Teutonic, American, English, German
- Deylin, Rhyming- a historical blacksmith with supernatural powers. Origin: English
- Idla, Battle. Origin: English
- Gylda, Gilded. Origin: English
- Cherrill, dear one; darling. Origin: English

- Burdette, Origin: English, French, American
- Lionel, Young lion. Origin: French, American, Latin, Arthurian Legend, English
- Alissa, Origin: English, American, Teutonic
- Barker, Shepherd. Origin: English
- Welsh, From Wales. Origin: English
- Udolph, Wealthy wolf. Origin: English
- Dalbert, Bright one; proud. Origin: English
- Ceapmann, Merchant. Origin: English
- Gene, Well born. Origin: Greek, American, English
- Kammie, Lord. Origin: Japanese, English
- Brittany, From Britain. Origin: Celtic, American, English
- Osbeorht, Divinely brilliant. Origin: English
- Aswinn, Friend with a spear. Origin: English
- Ocelfa, From the high plain. Origin: English
- Jackleen, the feminine of Jacques. Origin: English

- Athelstan, Name of a king. Origin: Anglo-Saxon, English
- Aekerman, Man of oak. Origin: English
- Martyn, Warrior of Mars. Origin: English, Latin
- Blythe, Happy, merry. Origin: English
- Vareck, From the fortress. Origin: English
- Atlea, From the meadow. Origin: English
- Raven, Raven. Origin: English
- Kaprisha, Caprice. Origin: English
- Audrina, Nobility; strength. Origin: English
- Geffrey, Peaceful. See also Jeffrey. Origin: English, French, Shakespearean
- Beall, Handsome. Origin: English, French
- Dent, Valley town. Origin: English
- Christy, From the Greek word meaning 'carrier of Christ', Origin: Greek, American, Irish, Scottish, English, Latin
- Brittanie, Origin: English, American
- Fairfax, Blond. Origin: Anglo-Saxon, English
- Austine, Origin: English, French, Latin
- Ashton, Town of ash trees. Origin: English, American

- Bavol, Wind. Origin: English
- Cale, Bold; Surname derived from Charles. Origin: English, American, Hebrew
- Byrn, Brook. Origin: English
- Kaitlynn, meaning pure. Origin: Irish, American
- Faerwald, Powerful traveler. Origin: English
- Temple, Origin: English, Latin
- Kendel, Royal valley. Surname referring to Kent in England. Origin: English
- Mace, A mace was a medieval weapon used by knights. Origin: English
- Abbott, Father. Origin: Hebrew, English
- Beceere, Lives by the beech tree. Origin: English
- Charleton, From Charles' farm. Origin: English
- Clarrie, A feminine name. Origin: English
- Bucky, Male deer. Origin: English, Greek
- Gilbert, Oath. Origin: Teutonic, American, Scottish, English, French, German, Welsh
- Barklay, Birch valley; birch tree meadow. Origin: English

- Wade, Moving. Origin: Anglo-Saxon, American, English, Scandinavian
- Dontae, Contemporary phonetic'enduring. Origin: English, American, Latin
- Bertilde, Shining battlemaid. Origin: English, Teutonic
- Kathy, Pure. Origin: English
- Brigbam, Lives by the bridge. Origin: English
- Hanford, From the high ford. Origin: English
- Danni, Feminine God will judge. Origin: English
- Lewis, Famous in war. Origin: Teutonic, American, French, English, Shakespearean
- Brett, Brit. A native of England: (Britain) Origin: English, French
- Ra, Doe. Origin: English
- Chasen, Huntsman. Origin: English
- Birley, From the cattle shed on the meadow. Origin: English
- Clemence. Origin: English, French, Latin
- Jonalyn, Modern feminine of John and Jon. Origin: English
- Averell, Wild boar. Origin: English
- Alisanne, Origin: English, French

- Thorne, From the thorn tree. Origin: English
- Varik, From the fortress. Origin: English, Teutonic
- Eadward, Guardian. Origin: Anglo-Saxon, English
- Chatham, From the soldier's land. Origin: English
- Gussie, A , Augustina, Augustine, or Augustus. Origin: English
- Daren, Great. Origin: English, Gaelic, American, African
- Bursone, Son of Byrne. Origin: English
- Elbertyna, Noble or glorious. Origin: English
- Brantson Mohawk Indian Joseph Brant was a renowned strategist who fought for the British during the... Origin: English
- Cissy, Origin: English
- Bemelle, Strong as a bear. Origin: English, German
- Quenton, fifth.' Surname. Origin: English, French
- Aud, Wealthy. Origin: Norse, English
- Bell, Handsome. Origin: French, English

- Tammie, Abbreviation of Thomasina and Tamara. Origin: English, American
- Barton, From the barley farm. Origin: English, American
- Deerborn, Deer river. Origin: English
- Charleson, A man. Origin: English
- Beverlee, Beaver stream. Origin: English, American
- Avalee, Origin: English
- Ifig, Ivy. Origin: English
- Avelina, given names Avis and Aveline. Origin: English
- Hline, From the bank. Origin: English
- Parnall, Little rock. Origin: English
- Kamryn, Modernused for girls. Origin: English, American
- Carynn, Modern. Origin: English
- Bradon, Broad hillside. Origin: English, Irish
- Pam, Name invented for a heroine of the book 'Arcadia. Origin: English, American
- Gale, Father rejoiced. Origin: Hebrew, American, English, Norse
- Ashlin, Lives at the ash tree pool. Origin: English
- Caro, Feminine manly. Origin: English

- Aethelisdun, From the noble's hill. Origin: English
- Faith, Confidence; trust; belief. Origin: Greek, Latin, American, English
- Danah, From Denmark. Origin: English
- Ciceron, Chickpea. Origin: Latin, Spanish, English
- Farron, English surname. Origin: English
- Geol, Born at Christmas. Origin: English
- Kandiss, Modern- ancient hereditary title used by Ethiopian queens. Origin: English
- Barlow, Lives on the bare hill. Origin: English
- Jonquil, From the flower name. Origin: English
- Hattie, Ruler of the home. Origin: Teutonic, American, English
- Berkley, The birch tree meadow. Also see Barclay and Burke. Origin: English, Irish
- Beadu, Warrior maid. Origin: English
- Jenaya, Modern name based on Jane or Jean. Origin: English
- Kaycie, Modern Kacie. Origin: English

- Chrissy, Abbreviation of Christine. Follower of Christ. Origin: Irish, Scottish, American, English
- Blakelee, From the light meadow; from the dark meadow. Origin: English
- Hod, Vigorous. Origin: Hebrew, English, Biblical
- Benjy, Right-hand son. Origin: English, Hebrew
- Darcy, Dark. Origin: Celtic, American, English, Irish, French
- Aescwyn, Spear friend. Origin: English
- Darcy, Dark. Origin: Irish, American, English, French
- Aetheston, From the noble's hill. Origin: English
- Jinny, Virgin. Origin: Latin, English
- Galen, Festive party. Origin: English
- Brocly, From the badger meadow. Origin: English
- Thorndike, From the thorny dike. Origin: English
- Zandra, defender of mankind. Origin: Spanish, English, Greek
- Abbot, Father. Origin: Hebrew, English
- Carla, Manly. Origin: Spanish, American, English, German
- Deems, Judge's son. Origin: English

- Linton, From the flax enclosure. Origin: English, American
- Laurian, From the place of laurel trees. Origin: English, Latin
- Birny, Small river or stream with an island. Origin: English
- Ada, First daughter. Origin: African, American, English, French, German, Hebrew, Teutonic
- Perkinson, Son of Perkin. Origin: English
- Lacee, Origin: English, French
- Burgiss, Citizen. Origin: English
- Egbertine, Shining sword. Origin: English
- Nicky, People's victory. Origin: Greek, American, English
- Beda, Warrior maid. Origin: English
- Igraine, Mother of Arthur. Origin: Arthurian Legend, English
- Nancie, meaning favor; grace. Origin: English, American, French
- Cleme, Gentle. Origin: English
- Alison, Son of All. Origin: English, Teutonic
- Jenalynn, Origin: English
- Candyce, ancient hereditary title used by Ethiopian queens. Origin: English
- Oldwin, Special friend. Origin: English

- Lenora, Shining light. Origin: English, American
- Eddison, Ed's son. Origin: Anglo-Saxon, English
- Burchard, Strong as a castle. Origin: English
- Chase, Huntsman. Origin: English, American
- Birch, Bright; shining; the birch tree. Origin: English
- Hughetta, Little Hugh. Origin: English
- Alexina, Defender of man. Origin: Latin, English, Greek
- Huntingtun, From the hunting farm. Origin: English
- Bruno, Dark skinned. Origin: Teutonic, American, Italian, English, German
- Wendall, Traveler; wanderer. Origin: English, German
- Laurene, Laurel. Origin: French, American, English, Latin
- Effie, Abbreviation of Greek name Euphemia meaning well spoken. Origin: English, American, Greek, Scottish
- Aldtun, From the old manor. Origin: English

- Ethel, noble. Origin: German, Hebrew, Teutonic, American, English
- Bertram, A knight. Origin: Arthurian Legend, American, Teutonic, English, German, Shakespearean
- Radolph, Red wolf. Origin: English
- Eadda, Wealthy. Origin: English
- Carmine, Song. Origin: English
- Auriar, Gentle music. Origin: English
- Jinni, Origin: English
- Benson, Ben's son. surname. Origin: English, Hebrew
- Bonie, Good. Origin: English
- Hlithtun, From tbe hillside town. Origin: English
- Charly. Manly. Origin: English
- Bromly, From the broom covered meadow. Origin: English
- Marsten, Town near the marsh. Origin: English
- Denni, Combination of Deana (divine) and Dina (from the valley; avenged). Origin: English
- Wainwright, Wagon maker. Origin: English
- Vallen, Strong. Origin: English, Latin
- Kapricia, Caprice. Origin: English

- Dawna, The first appearance of daylight; daybreak. Origin: English, American
- Camille, flower name Camelia. Origin: English, American, French, Latin
- Waerheall, From the true man's manor. Origin: English
- Averil, Wild boar. Origin: English, Anglo-Saxon
- Fullere, Cloth thickener. Origin: English
- Frayne, Foreigner. Origin: English
- Freda, Elf strength, good counselor. Origin: English, American, Teutonic, German, Welsh
- Bradburn, From the broad brook. Origin: English
- Shepard, Shepherd. Origin: Anglo-Saxon, English
- Alleyne, Fair; handsome. Also both a (noble, bright) and an abbreviation of names beginning with Al-. Origin: English
- Bartoli, Ploughman. Origin: Spanish, English
- Aethretun, Lives at the spring farm. Origin: English
- Budington, British place name. Origin: English
- Fuller, Cloth thickener. Origin: English

- Jonalynn, Modern feminine of John and Jon. Origin: English
- Brice, Speckled. Origin: Scottish, American, Anglo-Saxon, Celtic, English, French
- Bertie, Intelligent; Glorious raven. Origin: French, American, English
- Frasier, French town. Origin: English, Scottish
- Saeger, Seaman. Origin: English
- Alcott, From the old cottage. Origin: English
- Brewstere, Brewer. Origin: English
- Brook, Water; stream. Origin: English, American
- Delbert, Bright day; sunny day; proud; noble. Origin: English, American
- Brammel, Place name in Britain. Origin: English
- Alleyn, Fair; handsome. Also both a (noble, bright) and an abbreviation of names beginning with Al-. Origin: English
- Danise, Feminine God will judge. Origin: English
- Hamlyn, House or home. Introduced from Germany during the Norman

Conquest. Also used as a surname. Origin: English, German

- Clarinda, Beautiful. Origin: Spanish, French, Latin, English
- Deonne, Divine. Origin: English
- Emelyn, meaning labor. Origin: English, French
- Somerset, From the summer settlers. Origin: English, Shakespearean
- Clemens, Gentle. Origin: English, American, Danish
- Alhrik, Sacred ruler. Origin: English
- Ellsworth, Great man's home. Origin: English, American
- Burgtun, From the fortress town. Origin: English
- Galt, From the high ground. Origin: English
- Baylen, auburn-haired. Origin: English, French
- Ashtin, Ash tree. Origin: English
- Aindrea, Brave; Manly. Famous Bearer: Prince Andrew. Origin: English
- Bancroft, From the bean field. Origin: English
- Janie, Gift from God; Jehovah has been gracious. Origin: Hebrew, American, English

- Barklie, Birch valley; birch tree meadow. Origin: English
- Beaman, Beekeeper. Origin: English
- Teriana, meaning harvester. Origin: English
- Jeralyn, Modern blend of Jerry and Marilyn. Origin: English
- Broughton, From the fortress town. Origin: English
- Roderik, Famous ruler. Origin: English, German
- Farrs, Son of Farr. Origin: English
- Aelfraed, Elf counselor. Origin: English
- Brinly, Burnt wood. Origin: English
- Rodger, Famed spear. Origin: English, American
- Kadia, Rhyming, meaning pure. Origin: English
- Cherrie, The fruit-bearing cherry tree. Origin: English
- Cheresse, dear one; darling. Origin: English
- Hildie, Battle maid. Origin: English
- Berty, Bright light. Origin: English
- Botwolf, Herald wolf. Origin: English
- Odell, Wealthy. Origin: Anglo-Saxon, Norse, American, Irish, English

- Slayton, From the valley farm. Origin: English
- Hollie, The holly tree. Common name given Christmas girl babies. Origin: English, American
- Bradlie, Origin: English
- Burney, Lives on the brook island. Origin: English, Irish
- Branton, Origin: English
- Berne, Strong as a bear. Origin: English, German
- Burdett, Surname used as a given name. Origin: English, French
- Brainerd, Bold raven. Origin: English
- Davidsone, David's son. Origin: English
- Fawna, Young deer. Origin: English
- Kalani, The sky; chieftain. Origin: Hawaiian, American
- Aldred, Old advisor. Origin: Anglo-Saxon, English
- Eadmund, Happy defender. Origin: English
- Ashenford, River ford near ash trees. Origin: English
- Brocleah, From tbe badger meadow. Origin: English
- Laec, Lives near water. Origin: English

- Graham, Grain. Origin: Latin, American, Anglo-Saxon, English, Scottish, Teutonic
- Ricarda, Rules the home. Origin: Spanish, German, Teutonic, English, Italian
- Odwolf, Wealthy wolf. Origin: English
- Jilliann, Jove's child.from the masculine Julian. Origin: English
- Gram, Grain. Origin: Latin, Anglo-Saxon, English, Norse
- Kaycee, Modern Kacie. Origin: English, American
- Oldwyn, Special friend. Origin: English
- Channe, Young wolf. Origin: English, Irish
- Caroliana, Feminine manly. Origin: English
- Tallon, Tall. Origin: English
- Bethiar, House of God. Origin: English
- Claytin, Town by a clay bed. Origin: English
- Saeweard, Sea guardian. Origin: English
- Dannah, Judging. God will judge. Origin: Biblical, English
- Carolann, Feminine manly. Origin: English, American

- Aikin, Oaken. Origin: English
- Brent, Hilltop. Origin: Celtic, American, English
- Huntley, From the hunter's meadow. Origin: English
- Aurick, Noble leader. Origin: German, English
- Jimmie, Supplanter. Origin: English, American
- Edie, Happy warfare. Origin: English, American
- Bonde, Man of the land. Origin: English
- Milburn, Millstream, From the mill stream. Origin: English, American
- Azure, Sky-blue. Origin: English, French
- Aethelbeorht, Splendid. Origin: English
- Emelye, Origin: English
- Aldreda, From Ealdraed, meaning old counsel. Aldred was common before the Norman Conquest, Origin: English
- Osburt, Divinely brilliant. Origin: English
- Deke, Dusty one; servant. Origin: English, Greek
- Nanette, Grace. Origin: Hebrew, American, French, English
- Christoff, He who holds Christ in his heart. Origin: English

- Cherie, darling. Origin: English, American, French
- Brit, Man from Britain. Origin: English
- Barrett, Bear. Origin: Teutonic, American, English, German
- Audre, Noble strength. Origin: English
- Atwater, From the waterside. Origin: English
- Baden, Surname. Origin: English
- Geraldine, Capable with a spear. Origin: Teutonic, American, German, English
- Tami, Abbreviation of Thomasina and Tamara., Origin: English, American, Japanese
- Waer, Wary. Origin: English
- Bailey, Courtyard within castle walls. Origin: English, French, American
- Burle, Fortified. See also Berlyn. Origin: English
- Jade, Jewel. Origin: Spanish, American, English
- Brigham, From the village near a bridge. Origin: English
- Carmelo, Garden. Origin: English, American, Hebrew

- Alin Fair; handsome. Also both a (noble, bright) and an abbreviation of names beginning with Al-. Origin: English
- Benjimen, Right-hand son. Origin: English
- Radella, Elfin counselor. Origin: English
- Carlyle, From the protected tower. Origin: English, American
- Alix, Of the nobility. From the German Adalheidis meaning nobility, and the French Adeliz which is Origin: English, Greek, Teutonic, French
- Radbert, Red haired counselor. Origin: English
- Bayne, Bridge. Origin: English
- Brookes, Brook; stream. Origin: English
- Haslet, From the hazel tree land. Origin: English
- Gradon, Gray-haired: son of the Gray family; son of Gregory. Origin: English
- Aethelwine, Friend of the elves. Origin: English
- Thorley, Thorn wood/clearing; from Thor's meadow. Origin: English, Teutonic
- Eada, Wealthy. Origin: English

- Wentworth, From the white one's estate. Origin: English
- Rodge, Famed spear. Origin: English
- Ulfred, Wolf of peace. Origin: English
- Jazmaine, Modern; combination of Jocelyn and the musical term jazz. Origin: English
- Lauriano, From the place of laurel trees. Origin: English, Latin
- Bonny, Beautiful. Origin: Latin, American, English, French, Scottish
- Nearra, Nearest. Origin: English
- Eda, Wealthy. Origin: Anglo-Saxon, American, English, Greek, Norse
- Jenalee, Origin: English
- Osrid, Divine counselor. Origin: English
- Kendal, From the bright valley. Origin: Celtic, English
- Sadie, Princess. Origin: Hebrew, American, Spanish, English
- Averil, From the Old English Everild. Origin: English, Latin
- Bazyl, Royal; kingly. Origin: English
- Jimmi, Modern feminine of Jimmy. Origin: English
- Botewolf, Herald wolf. Origin: English

- Carrington, Place name and surname. Origin: Celtic, English
- Eadweald, Wealthy ruler. Origin: English
- Jaylene, Feminine. Origin: English, American
- Cherisa, dear one; darling. Origin: English
- Dalyn, Rhyming- a historical blacksmith with supernatural powers. Origin: English
- Chadwik, From the warrior's town. Origin: English
- Bates, often used as a surname. Origin: English, Shakespearean
- Clarrisa, or Clarice. Bright; shining and gentle; famous. Origin: English
- Daena, From Denmark. Origin: English
- Aenescumb, Lives in the valley of the majestic one. Origin: English
- Christina, Christian. Origin: Swedish, American, English, Latin
- Aekley, From the oak tree meadow. Origin: English
- Bartolomeo, Son of a farmer. Origin: English
- Caddaric, Battle leader. Origin: English
- Miller, One who grinds grain. Origin: English, American, Latin

- Irvine, Beautiful. Origin: Scottish, English
- Ellene, Means light or most beautiful woman. Origin: English
- Nick, People's victory. Origin: Greek, American, English
- Cissie, Origin: English
- Ailean, Fair; handsome. Famous Bearer: U.S. actor Alan Alda. Origin: English, Gaelic, Scottish
- Hamon, House or home. Origin: English, German
- Ives, Archer. Origin: Teutonic, English, German
- Sage, Wise one. Origin: English, French, American
- Carolyn Joy. Song of happiness. Also feminine manly. Origin: English, American, Italian
- Bayhard, Reddish brown hair. Origin: English
- Daisi, Day's eye. A flower name. Origin: English, French
- Cecillus, Blind, Origin: English
- Jaymes, Supplanter. Origin: English
- Carrol, Champion. Origin: Celtic, American, English

- Brett, A Breton. Origin: Celtic, American, English
- Albertine, noble. Origin: Spanish, American, Teutonic, German, English
- Smythe, Tradesman. Origin: English
- Thelma, Origin: English, American, Greek
- Danita, God has judged. Origin: Hebrew, American, English, Spanish
- Carol, Champion. Origin: Gaelic, American, English
- Bink, Lives at the bank. Origin: English
- Chilton, From the farm by the spring. Origin: English
- Aldis, From the old house. Origin: English
- Bercleah, Lives at the birch tree meadow. Origin: English
- Ravyn, Dark haired or wise. Origin: English
- Chatlie, Manly. Origin: English
- Jayron, like Jason and Jacob. Origin: English
- Burket, Area of birch trees. Origin: English
- Janetta, Gift from God. Origin: Hebrew, English, Scottish
- Brooklynne, Water; stream. Origin: English

- Gytha, Warlike. Origin: Norse, English, Danish
- Diamontina, Of high value; brilliant. Origin: English
- Hiatt, From the high gate. Origin: English
- Hartley, From the stag's meadow. Origin: English
- Ellie, Origin: French, American, English
- Dorian, Descendant of Dorus. Origin: English, American, Greek
- Isabelle, Devoted to God. Origin: Hebrew, American, Spanish, English
- Claudine, Feminine of Claude. Origin: English, German, American, French
- Ellery, Dwells by the alder trees. Origin: Teutonic, English, German, Greek
- Daly, Small valley. Abbreviation of Madeline. Origin: English
- Byrdene, Little bird. Origin: English
- Hallfrita, Peaceful home. Origin: English
- Avryl, Opening buds of spring; born in April. Origin: English
- Berwin, Harvest-time friend. Origin: English
- Braw)eigh, From the hillslope meadow. Origin: English
- Birky, Birch island. Origin: English

- Dawne, The first appearance of daylight; daybreak. Origin: English
- Margerie, French Margerie. Origin: English
- Orabel, Beautiful seacoast. Origin: English
- Paegastun, From the fighter's farm. Origin: English
- Balamy, Good-looking companion. Origin: English
- Akker, From the oak tree. Origin: English
- Brandyce, beverage brandy used as a given name. Origin: English
- Parisch, Lives near the church. Origin: English
- Aldys, From the old house. Origin: English
- Barrlow, Hillside. Origin: English
- Auden, Old friend. Origin: English
- Ally, A 13th centurymeaning nobility. Now particularly popular in Scotland.
- Bosworth, Lives at the cattle enclosure. Origin: English
- Albertyne, Intelligent. Origin: German, English
- Jacy, Moon. Origin: Native American, English

- Chrystina, Follower of Christ. Origin: English, Latin
- Raven. Origin: English
- Christa, Follower of Christ. Origin: English, Latin, American, Greek, Irish
- Elyta, Winged. Origin: English
- Hillock, From the small hill. Origin: English
- Chancey, Chancellor; secretary; fortune; a gamble. Origin: English
- Holbrook, From the brook. Origin: English
- Brandelyn, beverage brandy used as a given name. Origin: English
- Caldre, Cold brook. Origin: English
- Bond, Tied to the land. Origin: English
- Diamonique, The precious diamond stone. Origin: English
- Milward, Keeper of the mill. Origin: English
- Darel, Open. Origin: English
- Kaye, keeper of the keys; pure. Origin: English, American
- Bramwel, Place name in Britain. Origin: English

- Tedman, Wealthy defender. Origin: Anglo-Saxon, English, Teutonic
- Elwin, Elf-wise friend. Origin: English, American
- Daisey, Day's eye. A flower name. Origin: English, American
- Becki, Abbreviation of Rebecca. Origin: English
- Jonna, Modern feminine of John and Jon. Origin: English, American
- Beamen, Beekeeper. Origin: English
- Byreleah, From the cattle shed on the meadow. Origin: English
- Billie, Determination, strength. A nickname for William. Origin: English, American
- Brik, Bridge. Origin: English
- Baylie, Courtyard within castle walls. Origin: English, French
- Jae, Feminine. Origin: English
- Jacque, Origin: English, American
- Byrleigh, British place name. Origin: English
- Christanne, Follower of Christ. Origin: English
- Bradly, From the broad meadow. Origin: English, American

- Eddrick, Power and good fortune. Origin: English
- Blithe, Cheerful. Origin: English
- Hampton, Place-name and surname. Origin: English, American
- Arwin, Friend of the people. Origin: German, English
- Chace, Huntsman. Origin: English
- Perry, Origin: French, American, Welsh, Latin, Anglo-Saxon, English
- Sally, Princess. Origin: Hebrew, American, English
- Chris, Follower of Christ. Origin: English, American, Greek
- Brynly, Burnt wood. Origin: English
- Osric, Divine ruler. Origin: Anglo-Saxon, English, Teutonic
- Linwood, From the linden tree dell. Origin: English, American
- Byme, Bear; brown. Origin: English, Irish
- Derebourne, From the deer brook. Origin: English
- Jeric, Strong; gifted ruler. Blend of Jer- and Derrick. Origin: English
- Basilius, Royal; kingly. Origin: English, Dutch

- Hayden, From the hedged in valley. Origin: English, American, Teutonic, Welsh
- Bayley, Steward or public official; man in charge. Origin: English, French
- Bek, Brook. Origin: English
- Christof, He who holds Christ in his heart. Origin: English
- Beldan, Lives in the beautiful glen. Origin: English, Teutonic
- Jonette, Modern feminine of John and Jon. Origin: English
- Briannon, Strong. Origin: Celtic, English
- Thorntun, From the thorn tree farm. Origin: English
- Claegborne, From the clay brook. Origin: English
- Barthel, Son of a farmer. Origin: English
- Ellisha, Greek form of Elijah. Origin: English
- Rangey, From raven's island. Origin: English
- Tait, Happy. Origin: Norse, Swedish, English, Irish, Scandinavian
- Sonnie, Son. Origin: English
- Haslett, From the hazel tree land. Origin: English
- Kacy, vigorous. Origin: English, American

- Eadwine, Wealthy friend. Origin: English
- Avelina, Origin: English
- Galina, God shall redeem. Origin: Hebrew, English, Greek
- Sheply, From the sheep meadow. Origin: Anglo-Saxon, English
- Ivalyn, A climbing evergreen ornamental plant. Origin: English
- Davonna, Beloved. Feminine of David. Origin: English
- Beverlee, Beaver stream. Origin: English
- Cartwright, Builder of carts. Origin: English
- Ladd, Attendant. Origin: English
- Ascot, Lives at the east cottage. Origin: English
- Hurlbert, Army strong. Origin: English
- Aylward, Noble guardian/protector. Origin: English, Teutonic
- Davynn, Beloved. Feminine of David. Origin: English
- Haig, From the hedged enclosure. Origin: English, Armenian
- Holcomb, From the deep valley. Origin: English
- Devynn, Divine. Origin: English, French

- Giles, Kind. Origin: Latin, American, Greek, English, Gaelic
- Thoraldtun, From the thunder estate. Origin: English
- Farson, Son of Farr. Origin: English
- Hollis, Lives by the holly trees. Origin: English, American
- Claudio, Lame. Origin: English, Spanish, Latin, Shakespearean
- Millie, Servant for the temple. Origin: Latin, American, French, English, German
- Betia, House of God. Origin: English
- Bayarde, Brown hair. Origin: English
- Napier, In charge of royal linens. Origin: English
- Caspar, Wealthy man. Origin: English, Persian
- Chrissie, Abbreviation of Christine. Follower of Christ. Origin: Irish, Scottish, English
- Falcon, Surname relating to falconry. Origin: English
- Breneon, Mountain peak. Origin: English
- Gifuhard, Gift of bravery. Origin: English
- Farrun, English surname. Origin: English
- Estmund, Protected by God. Origin: English

- Deerward, Guardian of the deer. Origin: English
- Mildraed, Mild of strength. Origin: English
- Thornton, Town of thorns. Origin: English, Gaelic, American
- Bethan, meaning either oath of God, or God is satisfaction. Origin: Greek, Hebrew, English
- Blyth, Merry. Origin: English
- Hester, Origin: English, American, Greek, Persian
- Adalson, Son of All. Origin: English
- Teriann, meaning harvester. Origin: English
- Burtt, Bright light. Origin: English
- Faye, Confidence; trust; belief. Origin: English, American, French
- Brittan, Brit. A native of Brittany. Origin: English
- Raoul, Strong. Origin: Teutonic, English, French
- Melva, Ruler. Origin: Irish, American, Celtic, English
- Kay, Glory. Origin: Greek, American, French, Irish, Arthurian Legend,

English, Latin, Native American,Scandinavian

- Candiss, ancient hereditary title used by Ethiopian queens. Origin: English
- Alberta, Intelligent or noble. Origin: Teutonic, American, Hungarian, English, German
- Blithe, Happy, merry. Origin: English
- Birtel, From the bird hill. Origin: English
- Christabel, Follower of Christ. Origin: English, Latin
- Dorette, Gift. Origin: Greek, English
- Chad, Name of a saint. Origin: Anglo-Saxon, American, Celtic, English
- Dana, From Denmark. Origin: Danish, American, Celtic, English, Hebrew, Irish
- Christofer, He who holds Christ in his heart. Origin: English, German
- Biecaford, From the hewer's ford. Origin: English
- Beach, Close to beech trees. Origin: English
- Berwyk, From the barley grange. Origin: English
- Bensson, Ben's son. surname. Origin: English

- Lauryn, place of honor and victory. Origin: English, American, Latin
- Budd, Friend. Origin: English, American
- Birly, Cow pasture. Origin: English
- Udale, From the yew tree valley. Origin: English
- Barthelemy, Ploughman. Origin: Aramaic, English
- Caddawyc, From the warrior's town. Origin: English
- Aelfdane, Danish elf. Origin: English Aelfdene, From the elfin valley. Origin: English
- Cable, Ropemaker. An English surname. Origin: English
- Bucklie, Deer-grazing meadow. Origin: English
- Choncey, Fortune; a gamble. Origin: English, French
- Dantina, Feminine God will judge. Origin: English
- Kenley, From the king's meadow. Origin: English
- Burnell, Strong as a bear. Origin: English, German, American, French, Irish
- Aldric, Wise ruler. Origin: English

- Cadence, meaning a rhythmic flow of sounds. Origin: English, American, Irish, French, Latin
- Queenie, Queen. Origin: English, American, Teutonic
- Caindale, From the clear river valley. Origin: English
- Salhtun, Lives near the willow farm. Origin: English
- Chelsea, Port. Origin: Anglo-Saxon, American, English
- Billie, Nickname for William 'resolute protector'. Origin: English, American, German
- Haden, From the heath. Origin: English, American
- Weslee, Feminine of Wesley. Origin: English
- Parker, Keeper of the forest. Origin: English, American
- Levina, Derived from the Roman given name Levinia. Origin: Spanish, English
- Janella, Jehovah has been gracious; has shown favor. Origin: English
- Levene, Issh. Origin: English
- Audel, Old friend. Origin: English

- Rexton, chieftain; ruler.' Surname. Origin: English, Latin
- Barclay, From the birch meadow. Origin: Anglo-Saxon, English, Scottish
- Jiselle, Pledge. Phonetic spelling of Giselle. Origin: English
- Hartford, From the stag's ford. Origin: English
- Radford, From the red ford. Origin: English
- Alfrida, Elf counselor. Origin: English
- Zabrina, Form of Sabrina: a princess. Origin: English
- Sherbourn, From the clear brook. Origin: English
- Aveline, given names Avis and Aveline. Origin: English, French
- Egberta, Shining sword. Origin: English
- Chrystian, Follower of Christ. Origin: English
- Teri, meaning harvester. Origin: English, American
- Rashawn, Blend of Ray and Shawn. Origin: English, American
- Barney, Comfort. Origin: Hebrew, American, English
- Botolph, Wolf. Origin: English, German

- Atworth, Lives at the farmstead. Origin: English
- Briana, Strong. Origin: Irish, American, Celtic, English
- Bobbi, Modern. Origin: English, American
- Bothe, Herald. Origin: Norse, English
- Talbott, Tall. Origin: English
- Kendriek, Son of Harry. Origin: English
- Fulaton, From the people's estate. Origin: English
- Bentlie, From the meadow. Origin: English
- Fytch, Ermine. Origin: English
- Elwald, Old Welshman. Origin: English
- Janene, Origin: English
- Dale, Lives in the valley. Surname. Origin: English, American, Teutonic
- Granville, meaning big town. Origin: English, American, French
- Kacie, vigorous. Origin: English, American
- Aurick, Noble leader. Origin: German, English
- Huntington, From the hunting farm. Origin: English
- Ivo, Archer's bow. Origin: English, Teutonic, German

- Sherbourne, From the clear brook. Origin: English
- Roderick, Famous ruler. Origin: English, American, German, Teutonic
- Graeme, Grain. Origin: Latin, Anglo-Saxon, English, Scottish
- Leopold, Bold for his people. Origin: Teutonic, American, English, German
- Bentlea, From the meadow. Origin: English
- Carswell, Lives at the watercress spring. Origin: English
- Deeann, meaning divine. Origin: English, American
- Velouette, Soft. Origin: English
- Aelfraed, Sage. Origin: English
- Wendlesora, From Windsor. Origin: English
- Cindi, Abbreviation of Cynthia and Lucinda. Origin: English, American
- Elliston, 'My God is Jehovah. Origin: English
- Jan, Gift from God. Origin: Hebrew, American, Swedish, Polish, Dutch, Slavic, English

- Galeun, From the town on the high ground. Origin: English
- Chuck, A from the Old English 'ceorl' meaning man. Origin: English, American
- Irving, White. Origin: Celtic, American, Gaelic, English, Scottish
- Carrie, manly. Origin: English, American, Italian
- Benet, Right-hand son. Origin: English, Latin, French
- Deondra, Divine. Origin: English
- Georgie, meaning tiller of the soil, or farmer. Origin: English, American
- Northwode, From the north forest. Origin: English
- Bartleigh, From Bart's meadow. Origin: English
- Nyle, Champion. Origin: Celtic, Anglo-Saxon, English
- Bort, Fortified. Origin: English
- Basilio, noble. Origin: Spanish, Greek, English
- Burley, Lives at the castle's meadow. Origin: English, American, Teutonic
- Atwell, Lives by the spring/well. Origin: English

- Camellia, flower name Camelia. Origin: English
- Doran, Stranger. Origin: Celtic, English, Greek, Irish
- Rickey, Abbreviation of Richard 'powerful; strong ruler. Origin: English, American
- Burhbank, Lives on the castle's hill. Origin: English
- Norwin, Friend of the north. Origin: English
- Graegleah, From the gray meadow. Origin: English
- Jackie, God is gracious. Origin: English, American, Scottish
- Barhloew, Lives on the bare hill. Origin: English
- Farryn, Adventurous. Origin: English
- Jayme, Supplanter. Origin: English, American
- Aldrich, Sage. Origin: Teutonic, English, French
- Marwood, From the lake forest. Origin: English
- Rodes, Lives near the crucifix. Origin: English

- Wacfeld, From Wake's field. Origin: English
- Ash, Happy. Origin: Hebrew, English
- Garrick, Spear king. Origin: Teutonic, American, German, English
- Fars, Son of Farr. Origin: English
- Danna, Feminine God will judge. Origin: English, American
- Brian, Strong. Origin: Norse, American, Celtic, English, Welsh
- Cass, Wealthy man. Origin: English, Latin, Irish, Welsh
- Blake, Light; dark. Origin: English, American, Scottish
- Azurine, Sky-blue. Origin: English, French
- Burlie, British place name. Origin: English
- Atherton, From the town by a spring. Origin: English
- Bundy, Free. Origin: English
- Bailey, Steward or public official; man in charge. Origin: English, French, American
- Oralie, Golden. Origin: English, Latin
- Bradd, Broad; wide. Origin: English
- Farron, English surname. Origin: English

- Gray, Gray-haired. Origin: English
  Graysen
- Addy, Son of Adam: Man of the red earth. Origin: Hebrew, English
- Halsig, From Hal's island. Origin: English
- Ulvelaik, Wolf sport. Origin: English
- Denver, Green valley. Origin: English
- Milman, Mill worker. Origin: English
- Chay, man. Origin: English
- Kendell, Royal valley. Surname referring to Kent in England. Origin: English
- Edina, Wealthy. Origin: Anglo-Saxon, English, Scottish
- Cimberleigh, From the royal meadow. Origin: English
- Burch, Birch. Origin: English
- Hide, From the hide. Origin: English
- Caryl, Love. Origin: Welsh, American, French, English
- Brook, Lives by the stream. Origin: English, American
- Kaedee, Rhyming, meaning pure. Origin: English
- Fawne, Young deer. Origin: English
- Hetheclif, From the heath cliff. Origin: English
- Yule, Born at Christmas. Origin: English

- Lisa, Devoted to God. Origin: German, American, Hebrew, Greek, English
- Aethelhard, Brave. Origin: English
- Rodd, Famous ruler. Origin: English, German
- Ashlie, Meadow of ash trees. Origin: English, American
- Beale, Handsome. Origin: English, French
- Ceolbeorht, Seaman. Origin: English
- Martin, Warring. Origin: Spanish, American, English, Latin
- Eadger, Wealthy spear. Origin: English
- Farris, Rock. Origin: Greek, American, English
- Jonita, Modern feminine of John and Jon. Origin: English
- Dalene, Small valley. Abbreviation of Madeline. Origin: English
- Eadsele, From Edward's estate. Origin: English
- Braden, Salmon. Origin: Scottish, American, English, Irish
- Fawna, Young deer. Origin: English
- Donny, Brown-haired chieftain. Origin: Irish, American, Gaelic, English, Scottish
- Faber, Origin: English, Latin

- Barnet, Of honorable birth. Origin: English
- Gyldan, Gilded. Origin: English
- Barbary, Origin: English
- Farryn, Adventurous. Origin: English
- Bartleah, From Bart's meadow. Origin: English
- Caryl, Man. Origin: English
- Ned, Prosperous protector. Origin: French, American, English
- Lex, Defender of men. Origin: Greek, English
- Dedrick, Rules the people. Origin: Teutonic, American, Dutch, English, German
- Beamann, Beekeeper. Origin: English
- Austina, Origin: English, French, Latin
- Aethelwyne, Friend of the elves. Origin: English
- Talbert, Tall. Origin: English
- Casper, Treasure. Origin: Persian, American, English
- Jonnie, Modern feminine of John and Jon. Origin: English, American
- Peter, A rock or stone. Origin: Biblical, American, Greek, English, Shakespearean

- Bradene, From the broad valley. Origin: English
- Zackary, Origin: English, American
- Clare, Illustrious. Origin: Latin, American, English
- Beorhthilde, Shining battlemaid. Origin: English
- Ashburn, Lives near the ash tree brook. Origin: English
- Beacher, Lives by the beech tree. Origin: English
- Quentrell, fifth.' Surname. Origin: English, French
- Mariel, Origin: English
- Eadwyn, Wealthy friend. Origin: English, Anglo-Saxon
- Clemmie, Gentle. Origin: English
- Nickson, Abbreviation of Nicholas. Origin: English
- Geoffrey, God's peace. Origin: Teutonic, American, English, Anglo-Saxon, French, German
- Jenee, Modern name based on Jane or Jean. Origin: English
- Adney, Lives on the noble's island. Origin: English
- Erwyna, Friend of the sea. Origin: English

- Marven, Form of Mervin. Origin: English
- Bess, meaning either oath of God, or God is satisfaction. Origin: Greek, American, Hebrew, English
- Derica, Gifted ruler. Modern feminine of Derek. Origin: English
- Bocley, Lives at the buck meadow. Origin: English
- Benn, Abbreviation of Benjamin and Benedict. Origin: English
- Kendrik, Son of Harry. Origin: English, Scottish, Welsh
- Laurel, Laurel. Origin: French, American, English, Latin
- Nikki, Abbreviation of Nicole, meaning victory. Origin: English, American, Greek, Japanese
- Callyr, Lark. Origin: English
- Onslow, From the zealous one's hill. Origin: English
- Nico, Abbreviation of Nicholas. Origin: English, American
- Jackson, God has been gracious. Origin: Scottish, American, English
- Bureig. Lives on the brook island. Origin: English
- Kailey, pure. Origin: English, American

- Alfredo, Sage; wise; elvin. Origin: English, American, Italian, Spanish
- Arvis, The people's friend. Origin: English
- Oleda, Winged. Origin: English
- Bobbie, Abbreviation of Robert. Origin: English, American, German
- Bryanna, Strong. Origin: Irish, American, Celtic, English
- Clayton, meaning clay and 'tun'.. Origin: English, American, Teutonic
- Birket, Area of birch trees. Origin: English
- Burgeis, Lives in town. Origin: English
- Churchyll, Lives at the church hill. Origin: English
- Farrun, English surname. Origin: English
- Katie, Pure. Origin: English, Greek, American, Irish
- Jacki, Origin: English
- Backstere, Baker. Origin: English
- Mae, Bitter. Origin: Hebrew, American, Anglo-Saxon, English, French
- Bourne, From the brook. Origin: English
- Baker, Baker. Origin: English
- Bard, Minstrel; a singer-poet. Origin: Celtic, English, Gaelic, Irish, Norse
- Barbra, Dry. A flower name. Origin: Greek, American, English

- Gabi, Woman of God. Origin: French, Italian, English
- Yardly, From the enclosed meadow. Origin: English
- Jeran, Modern Jaron 'cry of rejoicing. Origin: English
- Neely, Feminine of Neil, meaning champion. Origin: English, Gaelic
- Elden, From the elves'valley 'From the old town.' Origin: English, American, Teutonic
- Nygel, Champion. From the Irish and Scottish Niall. Origin: English, Scandinavian, Gaelic
- Arwyn, Friend of the people. Origin: German, English
- Lacina, Origin: English, French
- Paella, Mantle. Origin: English
- Blostm, Fresh. Origin: English
- Bryani, The name of a flowering vine used in folk medicine. Origin: English, Greek
- Braedon, Broad hillside. Origin: English, Irish, American
- Averel, Fighting boar. Origin: English
- Odale, Of the valley. Origin: English

- Bretton, Man from Britain. Origin: English, Scottish
- Burhford, Lives at the castle ford. Origin: English
- Holdyn, From the hollow in the valley. Origin: English
- Thomdic, From the thorny dike. Origin: English
- Britt, Man from Britain. Origin: English, American, Dutch
- Indiana, The country India. Origin: English
- Frankie, meaning from France, or free one. Origin: Latin, American, English, French
- Alexa, Defender of man. Origin: Hungarian, American, English, Greek
- Kaitlyn, meaning pure. Origin: Irish, American
- Briseida, Origin: English
- Lacyann, Origin: English, French
- Beverley, Beaver stream. Origin: English
- Kandy, Modern- ancient hereditary title used by Ethiopian queens. Origin: English, American
- Diamond, Of high value; brilliant. Origin: English, American
- Cissy, Origin: English

- Eadburt, Wealthy. Origin: English
- Candace, Who possesses contrition. Origin: Biblical, American, English, Hebrew, Latin
- Audrianna, Nobility; strength. Origin: English
- Carolynn, Feminine manly. Origin: English, American
- Ellwood, From the old forest. Origin: English, American
- Madelena, From the tower. Origin: Hebrew, English
- Esrlson, Nobleman's son. Origin: English
- Jerard, Rules by the spear.' English surname. Origin: English, French
- Laefertun, From the rush farm. Origin: English
- Elvyne, Good elf. Origin: English
- Cherisse, dear one; darling. Origin: English
- Maralyn, Blend of Marie or Mary and Lyn. Origin: English
- Audriana, Nobility; strength. Origin: English
- Ashbey, Ash tree farm. Origin: English
- Barthram, Glorious raven. Origin: English

- Ben, Right-hand son. Origin: English, American, Biblical, Hebrew, Latin
- Melodie, Melody. Origin: English, French, American, Greek
- Hughie, Heart. Mind. Inspiration. Intelligent. Origin: English, American, Welsh
- Kaelah, The laurel crown. Origin: Israeli, English
- Barwolf, Ax wolf. Origin: English
- Bardrick, Ax ruler. Origin: English, German
- Benecroft, From the bean field. Origin: English
- Norward, Northern guardian. Origin: English, Teutonic
- Ora, Light. Origin: Hebrew, American, Spanish, Latin, Anglo-Saxon, English
- Dagian, Dawn. Origin: English
- Neddie, Prosperous protector. Origin: French, English
- Devonne, Divine. Origin: English, French
- Azura, Blue. Origin: Persian, English, French
- Bradan, From the broad valley. Origin: English
- Kadin, Companion. Origin: Arabic, American

- Bell, White. Origin: Czechoslovakian, American, English, French, German, Latin, Spanish
- Kaelyn, pure. Origin: English, American
- Claiborne, Stream by a clay bed. Origin: English
- F'enton, From the farm on the fens. Origin: English
- Burbank, Lives on the castle's hill. Origin: English
- Tacy, Silence. Also an abbreviation of Anastacia. Origin: English, Latin
- Aubrey, Rules with elf-wisdom. Origin: English, French, American
- Wessley, West meadow.English surname Westley. Origin: English
- Osmarr, Divinely glorious. Origin: English
- Beverly, Woman from the beaver meadow. Origin: English, American
- Quinton, Born fifth. Origin: Latin, American, English, French
- Dale, Lives in the valley. Small valley. Surname. Origin: English, American, Norse
- Dennis, Follower of Dionysius (Greek god of wine). Origin: Greek, American, French, English, Shakespearean

- Callie, Lark. Origin: English, American, Greek, Gaelic, Irish
- Bertilda, Shining battlemaid. Origin: English, Teutonic
- Wendy, Family; Wanderer. Origin: German, American, English
- Mildrid, Mild of strength. Origin: English
- Kayce, Modern Kacie. Origin: English
- Roddrick, Famous ruler. Origin: English, German
- Ashleena, Meadow of ash trees. Origin: English
- Diamont, Bridge protector. Origin: English
- Bridge, Lives near a bridge. Origin: English
- Orabelle, Beautiful seacoast. Origin: English
- Aymer, noble. Origin: English
- Thorn, Town of thorns. Thornton variant. Surname. Origin: English
- Dannee, Feminine God will judge. Origin: English
- Bardaric, Ax ruler. Origin: English
- Brown, Brown (colour name). Origin: English, American
- Cherese, dear one; darling. Origin: English

- Yedda, Beautiful voice. Origin: English
- Hugi, Intelligent. Origin: English, Norse
- Mindie, Abbreviation of Melinda. Origin: English
- Cherice, dear one; darling. Origin: English
- Athmore, From the moor. Origin: English
- Calfhierde, Shepherd. Origin: English
- Hamo, House or home. Origin: English, German
- Valiant, Brave. Origin: English, French
- Briggebam, Lives by the bridge. Origin: English
- Chaunceler, Chancellor. Origin: English
- Aldrik, Noble friend. Origin: German, English
- Birdie, Little bird; birdlike. Origin: English, American
- Quincey, Fifth. Derived from Roman clan name. Origin: English, French
- Maci, Derived from medieval male form of Matthew. Origin: English, American
- Brentan, From the steep hill. Origin: English
- Alarice, Rules all. Feminine of Alaric. Origin: English, German

- Aston, From the eastern town. Origin: English
- Unity, Together. Origin: Irish, English
- Tadd, Father. Origin: Welsh, English
- All, wise, Origin: English
- Fugeltun, From the people's estate. Origin: English
- Laverne, Woodland. Origin: French, American, English
- Parnell, Origin: English, Irish
- Graeghamm, From the gray home. Origin: English
- Aescford, Lives by the ash tree ford. Origin: English
- Geoff, Peaceful gift. Origin: Anglo-Saxon, English, French
- Temple, Temple-town. Origin: English
- Chap, Peddler; merchant. Origin: English
- Roddric, Famous ruler. Origin: English, German
- Barlowe, Hillside. Origin: English
- Cathy, 'pure'. Origin: Greek, American, French, Latin, Irish, English
- Osred, Divine counselor. Origin: English
- Rickman, Powerful. Origin: English
- Skyelar, Phonetic spelling of Schuyler. Origin: English

- Bret, From Britain. Origin: Celtic, English, French
- Cathie, pure. Origin: English, American
- Hugo, Intelligent. Origin: Spanish, Swedish, Teutonic, American, English, German, Latin
- Ashbie, Ash tree farm. Origin: English
- Erving, Beautiful. Origin: Scottish, English
- Waite, Guard. Origin: English
- Gillot, origin of the term 'to jilt', Origin: English
- Dora, Origin: English, American, Greek, Latin
- Joni, Modern feminine of John and Jon. Origin: English, American
- Bartlet, Ploughman. Son of Talmai. Origin: Hebrew, English
- Barnham, From the baron's home. Origin: English
- Blondelle, Fair-haired; blonde.Spanish Blandina meaning flattering. Origin: English, French
- Quentin, Born fifth. Origin: Latin, American, English, French
- Branhard, Bold raven. Origin: English

- Burkhart, Strong as a castle. Origin: German, English
- Kayanna, keeper of the keys; pure. Origin: English
- Birdy, Birdlike. Origin: English
- Haddon, From the heath. Origin: English
- Unwin, Unfriendly. Origin: English
- Avryll, Fighting boar. Origin: English
- Jo, Origin: English, American, French, Latin
- Hatty, Ruler of the home. Origin: Teutonic, English
- Dallin, Proud. Origin: English, American, Irish
- Janice, Gift from God. Origin: Hebrew, American, English
- Ivey, A climbing evergreen ornamental plant. Origin: English, American
- Faulkner, Falconer; one who trains falcons. Origin: English
- Bobby, Abbreviation of Robert. Origin: English, American, German
- Burton, From the fortified town. Origin: English, American
- Chaz, a man. Origin: English, American
- Alexine, Defender of man. Origin: Latin, Greek, English
- Alburt, Noble or bright. Origin: English

- Beal, Handsome. Origin: English, French
- Bradfurd, Broad stream. Origin: English
- Ainslie, Derived from the Brittish Nottinghamshire. Origin: English
- Hartwell, Lives near the stag's spring. Origin: English, Teutonic
- Benett, Right-hand son. Origin: English
- Aethelberht, Noble or bright. Origin: English
- Aeldra, Noble. Origin: English
- Neddy, Prosperous protector. Origin: French, English
- Parkins, Son of Parkin. Origin: English
- Barth, Son of the earth. Origin: English
- Braydon, Broad hillside. Origin: English, Irish, American
- Kailee, pure. Origin: English, American
- Jered, rules by the spear. Origin: English, American, Biblical
- Erwina, Friend of the sea. Origin: English
- Brucie, Thick brush. Origin: English
- Beldene, Lives in the beautiful glen. Origin: English
- Aethelstun, From the elfs home. Origin: English
- Adken, Oaken. Origin: English
- Blayr, Flatland. Origin: English

- Al, Friend. Origin: German, American, Celtic, English, Gaelic
- Kamron, Modernused for girls. Origin: English
- Eadgar, An Old English name meaning rich or happy. Origin: English
- Eadbeorht, Wealthy. Origin: English
- Nancey, meaning favor; grace. Origin: English, French
- Peyton, royal. Origin: Scottish, American, Latin, Irish, English
- Berwick, From the barley grange. Origin: English
- Brainard, Bold raven. Origin: English, Teutonic
- Nortin, From the north farm. Origin: English
- Autumn, Born in the fall; The fall season. Origin: English, American
- Janell, Jehovah has been gracious; has shown favor. Origin: English, American
- Brand, Firebrand. Origin: Norse, English, German
- Alen, Fair; handsome. Also both a (noble, bright) and an abbreviation of names beginning with Al-. Origin: English

- Brynley, Burnt wood. Origin: English
- Marston, From the farm by the pool 'Town near the marsh. Origin: English
- Ciss, Origin: English
- Nann, meaning favor; grace. Origin: English, French
- Lisandra, Defender of mankind. Feminine of Alexander. Origin: English, Greek
- Benedick, Origin: English, Latin, Shakespearean
- Aubrey, Rules with elf-wisdom. Origin: English, American, French, Teutonic
- Blane, Origin: English, Scottish, American, Celtic, Gaelic
- Adkins, Son of Aiken. Origin: English
- Atilda, At the elder tree. Origin: English
- Braxton, Brock's town. Origin: English, American
- Allen, Harmony, stone, or noble. Also fair, handsome. Originally a saint's name. Origin: Celtic, American, English
- Aeldra, Lives at the elder tree. Origin: English
- Charlyn, Manly. Origin: English
- Cicily, Origin: English

- Ave, Fighting boar. Origin: English
- Jenelle, Origin: English, American
- Black, Dark. Origin: English
- Halstead, From the manor house. Origin: English
- Hern, Mythical hunter. Origin: English
- Aelfwine, Friend of the elves. Origin: English
- Sallsbury, From the fortified keep. Origin: English
- Hew, Heart. Mind. Inspiration. Intelligent. Origin: English
- Tamsin, Twin'. Origin: English
- Ain, An hour, eye, fountain. Origin: Biblical, English
- Bradbourne, From the broad brook. Origin: English
- Beval, Like the wind. Origin: English
- Clerk, Scholar. Origin: English
- Defena, From Devonshire. Origin: English
- Beverley, Beaver stream. Origin: English, American
- Wake, Alert. Origin: English
- Banjamon, Right-hand son. Origin: English
- Christyn, Follower of Christ. Origin: English

- Franklynn, Free land-owner. Origin: English
- Ava, Iniquity. Origin: Biblical, American, English, Latin
- Birnie, Small river or stream with an island. Origin: English
- Ervine, Friend. Origin: English
- Byrley, British place name. Origin: English
- Clemency. Origin: English, Latin
- Rad, Red. Origin: English
- Temperance, Temperance. Origin: English
- Egbertyne, Shining sword. Origin: English
- Dianda, Deanne (divine). Origin: English
- Daviot, Beloved. Origin: English
- Lenny, Abbreviation of Leonard. Origin: English, American, German
- Carolan, Feminine manly. Origin: English, Irish
- Parkin, Little rock. Origin: English
- Dawn, Awakening. Origin: Anglo-Saxon, American, English
- Yetta, Generous. Origin: English, American

- Dorit, meaning Gift of God. Origin: English
- Austen, Origin: French, American, English
- Kandis, Modern- ancient hereditary title used by Ethiopian queens. Origin: English
- Nickie, Abbreviation of Nicole, meaning victory. Origin: English
- Carola, Joy. Origin: Spanish, English, French
- Blagdan, From the dark valley. Origin: English
- Lacy, Origin: English, American, French
- Jayne, Gift from God. Origin: Hebrew, American, Hindi, Sanskrit, English
- Melbyrne, From the mill stream. Origin: English
- Snowden, From the snowy hill. Origin: English
- Wait, Guard. Origin: English
- Aldo, Archaic. Origin: English, American, German, Italian, Teutonic
- Hlynn, Waterfall. Origin: English
- Bocleah, Lives at the buck meadow. Origin: English
- Hartun, From the gray estate. Origin: English

- Blakemore, From the dark moor. Origin: English
- Calldwr, Cold brook. Origin: English
- Brittney, Origin: English, American
- Palmer, Pilgrim; bearing a palm branch. Origin: English, American, Latin
- Liz, meaning either oath of God, Origin: Hebrew, American, Greek, English
- Danon, from Denmark. Origin: English
- Irven, White. Origin: Celtic, English
- Meldrick, From the powerful mill. Origin: English
- Farun, Origin: English
- Brittain, Brit. A native of Brittany. Origin: English
- Adalbeorht, noble. Origin: English
- Roger, Famous fighter. Origin: Teutonic, American, English, German, Shakespearean
- Kelvin, From the narrow river. Origin: Celtic, Gaelic, American, English
- Albrecht, Intelligent or noble. Origin: German, English
- Audric, Old or wise ruler. Origin: French, English, German
- Bardene, From the boar valley. Origin: English

- Aldus, From the old house. Origin: English, German
- Claressa, or Clarice. Bright; shining and gentle; famous. Origin: English
- Baldwin, Noble friend. Origin: Teutonic, German, English
- Lauretta, symbols of honour and victory. Origin: Latin, American, English
- Sherri, darling or dear one. Origin: English, American
- Avrill, Fighting boar. Origin: English
- Burrell, Fortified. See also Berlyn. Origin: English, American, French
- Haven, Place of safety; shelter. Origin: English
- Davy, Cherished; Beloved. Origin: Hebrew, American, Scottish, Welsh, English, Shakespearean
- Ava, Iniquity. Origin: Biblical, American, English, Latin
- Bonds, Man of the land. Origin: English
- Jereth, Bled of Jar or Jer and Gareth. Origin: English
- Hawley, From the hedged meadow. Origin: English
- Cadyna, Rhythmic. Origin: English
- Allison, A 13th centurymeaning nobility. Now particularly popular in Scotland.

Origin: French, American, English, Irish, Teutonic
- Tal, Tall. Origin: English, Israeli
- Alberto, Old English for brilliant; bright. Origin: English, American, Spanish
- Brooksone, Son of Brooke. Origin: English
- Wadsworth, From Wade's estate. Origin: English
- Imogen, Innocent. Last born. Origin: English, Irish, Latin, Shakespearean
- Castel, Castle. Origin: English
- Tempeltun, From the temple farm. Origin: English
- Jadrien, Blend of Jay or Jade and Adrien. Origin: English
- Christan, Follower of Christ. Origin: English
- Nan, Grace. Origin: Hebrew, American, French, English
- Banaing, Son of the slayer. Origin: English
- Bromleigh, From the broom covered meadow. Origin: English
- Meldrik, From the powerful mill. Origin: English
- Erwinek, Boar-friend. Origin: English

- Bartram, Glorious raven. Origin: German, Danish, English, Teutonic
- Franklyn, Free man; landholder. Origin: English, American
- Ranfield, From the raven's field. Origin: English, Rang
- Gildan, Gilded. Origin: English
- Hank, Rules an estate. Origin: Teutonic, American, German, Dutch, English
- Blayre, Flatland. Origin: English
- Barre, Gateway. Origin: English
- Ogden, From the oak tree valley. Origin: English
- Banbrigge, Lives near the bridge over the white water. Origin: English
- Carthage, Loving. Origin: Irish, Welsh, English
- Kaela, The laurel crown. Origin: Israeli, American
- Fraser, French town. Origin: English, Scottish
- Dee, Dark. Origin: Welsh, American, English
- Bruce, Thick brush. Origin: English, American, French, Scottish
- Allon, Fair; handsome. Also both a (noble, bright) and an abbreviation

of names beginning with Al-. Origin: English, Biblical, Hebrew
- Kandace, ancient hereditary title used by Ethiopian queens. Origin: English, American
- Charity, Benevolent goodwill and love. Origin: English, American, French, Latin
- Biron, Origin: English
- Edelmar, noble. Origin: English
- Blaec, Black or white. Origin: English
- Beorhthramm, Glorious raven. Origin: English
- Jerick, Strong; gifted ruler. Blend of Jer- and Derrick. Origin: English
- Wain, Craftsman. Origin: English
- Brucey, Thick brush. Origin: English
- Charlee, Manly. Origin: English
- Cherri, The fruit-bearing cherry tree. Origin: English, American
- Clarissa, Clear. Origin: Italian, Spanish, American, English, Latin
- Barnett, Baronet; leader. Origin: English
- Zackery. Origin: English, American
- Francie, From France or 'free one.' Feminine of Francis. Origin: Latin, English

- Edbert, Wealthy. Origin: English
- Elwood, From the old forest. Origin: English, American
- Carmya, Song. Origin: English
- Brandilyn, beverage brandy used as a given name. Origin: English
- Averil, Wild boar. Origin: English, Anglo-Saxon
- Daizy, Day's eye. A flower name. Origin: English
- Hilton, From the hall on the hill. Origin: English, American
- Charmaine, Song. Origin: English, American, French
- Aenedleah, From the awe inspiring one's meadow. Origin: English
- Byrd, Bird. Origin: English, American
- Aisley, Lives in the ash tree grove. Origin: English
- Cerella, Mistress; lady. Feminine of Cyril. Origin: English
- Diamante, Of high value; brilliant. Origin: English
- Brooklynn, Water; stream. Origin: English, American
- Huntly, From the hunter's meadow. Origin: English

- Shelton, From the ledge farm 'Deep valley. Origin: English, American
- Alain, Harmony, stone, or noble. Origin: Celtic, English, Arthurian Legend, French
- Nicol, People's victory. Origin: Greek, English, Scottish
- Zakary, and Zachary. Origin: English, American
- Baul, Snail. Origin: English
- Sherborne, From the clear brook. Origin: English
- Aerwyna, Friend of the sea. Origin: English
- Bradshaw, broad clearing in the wood. Origin: English
- Gilmar, Famous hostage. Origin: English
- Eadwine, Wealthy friend. Origin: English
- Leoma, Bright. Origin: English
- Marie, Bitter. Origin: English, French, American, Hebrew
- Ogelsvy, Fearsome. Origin: English
- Nikos, Abbreviation of Nicholas. Origin: English
- Jenai, God has answered. 'Origin: English
- Shelley, From the ledge meadow. Origin: Anglo-Saxon, English

- Kaycie, Origin: English
- Gaarwine, Friend with a spear. Origin: English
- Davion, Beloved. Origin: English, American
- Bertha, Sparkling. Origin: Teutonic, American, English, German
- Kaprice, Caprice.Origin: English
- Frisa, Curly - haired. Origin: English
- Ailin, Fair; handsome. Famous Bearer: U.S. actor Alan Alda. Origin: English, Gaelic, Irish
- Carmita, Song. Origin: English, Spanish
- Clare, Bright. Origin: French, American, Latin, English
- Rolf, Wolf. Origin: Norse, Swedish, American, English, Teutonic, German
- Cadee, meaning a rhythmic flow of sounds. Origin: English, Irish
- Dorcey, Dark. Origin: English
- Tedric, Abbreviation of Theodore. Origin: English
- Elbertina, noble. Origin: Spanish, English
- Adny, Lives on the noble's island. Origin: English
- Farron, Adventurous. Origin: English

- Jeremie, in use since the Middle Ages. Origin: English, American, Hebrew
- Aldn'd, Wise or red haired man. Origin: English
- Chatwin, Warring friend. Origin: English
- Dorita, Origin: English, Greek
- Albertyna, noble. Origin: English
- Odayle, Of the valley. Origin: English
- Burn, From the brook. Origin: English
- Norwell, From the north spring. Origin: English
- Banjamino, Right-hand son. Origin: English
- Emblem, meaning labor. Origin: English, French
- Ailis, noble. Origin: Celtic, German, Gaelic, English, Irish
- Baerhloew, Ruler or lives on the bare hill. Origin: English
- Charla, Feminine manly. Origin: English, American
- Dontrell, Contemporary phonetic'enduring. Origin: English
- Christmas, Origin: English
- Rawgon, Son of Rawley or Raleigh. Origin: English

- Blaze, Stutters. Origin: English, American, French, Latin
- Bromley, From the broom covered meadow. Origin: English
- Wendale, Traveler; wanderer. Origin: English, German
- Diandra, Divine. Origin: French, English
- Tennyson, Son of Dennis. Origin: English
- Ogelsvie, Fearsome. Origin: English
- Ilene, Origin: English, American
- Halsey, From Hal's island. Origin: English
- Adalbrechta, noble. Origin: English
- Avah, Origin: English
- Benji, Right-hand son. Origin: English
- Banning, Little blond one. Origin: Gaelic, English, Anglo-Saxon
- Vail, Lives in the valley. Origin: English, French
- Blyss, Joy. Cheer. Origin: English
- Hallie, From the Hall. Origin: English, American, Teutonic
- Norvin, From the north. Origin: Teutonic, English
- Bridger, Lives near a bridge. Origin: English, American
- Hayes, Surname. Origin: Irish, American, English

- Burghard, Strong as a castle. Origin: English
- Dannalee, Feminine God will judge. Origin: English
- Audie, Noble strength. Origin: English, American
- Channon, Young wolf. Origin: English, Irish
- Roe, Red haired. Origin: Anglo-Saxon, American, English
- Jerelyn, Modern blend of Jerry and Marilyn. Origin: English
- Holly, From the plant name. Holy. Origin: English, American, French
- Blayne, Origin: Scottish, Celtic, English
- Edgardo, Wealthy man holding a spear. Origin: English, American, Spanish
- Hayle, Lives in the hall. Origin: English
- Jim, Supplanter. Origin: Hebrew, American, English
- Christopher, He who holds Christ in his heart. Origin: English, American, Latin, Greek, Shakespearean
- Brockley, From the badger meadow. Origin: English
- Dalwin, Friend; good friend. Origin: English

- Circehyll, Lives at the church hill. Origin: English
- Deorward, Guardian of the deer. Origin: English
- Ullock, Wolf sport. Origin: English
- Burl, Forest; cup bearer. Origin: English, American
- Bayard, auburn-haired. Origin: English, French, Teutonic
- Golding, Son Of Gold. Origin: English
- Bryden, Place name in Britain. Origin: English
- Frank, Free. Origin: Teutonic, American, Latin, French, English
- Bryann, Strong. She ascends. Feminine of Brian. Origin: Celtic, English
- Sonny, Son. Origin: English, American
- Garr, Spear. Origin: Anglo-Saxon, English
- Kacey, Origin: English, American
- Buckly, Deer-grazing meadow. Origin: English
- Dain, Brook. Origin: English, Norse, Scandinavian
- Tegan, Beautiful. Origin: Welsh, English, Irish
- Bitanig, From the preserving land. Origin: English

- Buckley, Boy. Origin: Irish, English
- Kacey, Origin: English
- Vale, Lives in the valley. Origin: English
- Smedley, From the flat meadow. Origin: English
- Claresta, Brilliant. Origin: English
- Fabian, Origin: English, American, Latin, Shakespearean, Swedish
- Rhodes, A rose. Origin: Biblical, English
- Deeandra, meaning divine. Origin: English
- Gann, Spear protector. Origin: English
- Ashly, Lives in the ash tree grove. Origin: English
- Bartholomew, Son of a farmer. Origin: English, American, Biblical, Hebrew
- Adam, The Biblical Adam is the English language equivalent., Origin: Muslim, American, Biblical, English, Hebrew
- Dania, God is my judge. Origin: Hebrew, American, English
- Brant, Firebrand. Origin: Teutonic, American, English
- Eth, meaning noble. Origin: English

- Alan, Fair; handsome. Famous Bearer: U.S. actor Alan Alda. Origin: English, American, Celtic
- Bellamy, Handsome. Origin: French, English
- Ellston, From the farm. Origin: English
- Pamelia, Name invented for a heroine of the book 'Arcadia'. Origin: English
- Bardarik, Ax ruler. Origin: English
- Jenevieve, Modern phonetic. Origin: English
- Wacuman, Watchman. Origin: English
- Madison, strong fighter. Origin: English, American, Teutonic
- Baynebridge, Bridge. Origin: English
- Velvet, Soft. Origin: English, American
- Caralyn, Feminine manly. Origin: English
- Adler, Brave noble. Origin: Teutonic, English, German
- Kadi, Rhyming, meaning pure. Origin: English
- Berwyn, Harvest-time friend. Origin: English, Welsh
- Denton, From the valley farm. Origin: English
- Shelly, Meadow on a ledge. Origin: English, American

- Tempestm, Turbulent; stormy. Origin: English
- Katrina, Pure. Origin: English, Finnish, German, Scandinavian, Swedish, American, Greek
- Miles, Servant. Origin: Irish, American, English, Latin, Greek, Hebrew
- Gifford, Brave. Origin: Teutonic, English, French
- Osborne, Divine bear. Origin: Norse, American, English
- Park, Of the forest. Origin: English, American
- Garnett, Armed with a spear. Origin: English, American
- Hadwin, War friend. Origin: English, Teutonic
- Claribel, Bright. Origin: French, American, Latin, English
- Brannt, Proud. Origin: English
- Tad, Father. Origin: Welsh, American, English
- Aubry, Rules with elf-wisdom. Origin: English, French
- Banner, Flag; ensign bearer. Origin: English, Scottish
- Terell, Powerful. Origin: English, German

- Burges, Citizen. Origin: English
- Brentley, Hilltop. Origin: Celtic, English
- Ainslie, Derived from the Brittish Nottinghamshire. Origin: English
- Clarice, ALatin Clara, meaning bright or clear. Origin: English, American, French, Latin
- Ellison, Greek form of Elijah. Origin: English
- Kenisha, Feminine, meaning royal obligation;clear water. Origin: English, American
- Sherlock, Blond. Origin: English
- Kendryk, Son of Harry. Origin: English
- Jenene, Origin: English
- Janey, Jehovah has been gracious Jehovah has shown favour, Origin: English, American
- Brougher, Lives at the fortress. Origin: English
- Carroll, Manly. Origin: Irish, American, Celtic, Gaelic, English
- Blythe Happy. Origin: Anglo-Saxon, English
- Christoforus, He who holds Christ in his heart. Origin: English
- Caroll, Man. Origin: English

- Cinwell, Lives at the king's spring. Origin: English
- Lauriel, sweet bay tree symbolic of honor and victory.
- Dekle, Dusty one; servant. Origin: English, Greek
- Birdhill, From the bird hill. Origin: English
- Hlink, From the bank. Origin: English
- Cleon, From the cliff. Origin: English, American, Greek, Shakespearean
- Christena, Follower of Christ. Origin: English, Latin, American
- Lionell, Young lion. Origin: English, French
- Jon, gracious; has shown favor. Origin: English, American, French, Hebrew
- Briannah, Strong. Origin: Celtic, English
- Nijel, Champion. From the Irish and Scottish Niall. Origin: English, Scandinavian, Gaelic
- Kady, meaning 'a rhythmic flow of sounds. Origin: English, Irish
- Cinda, Abbreviation of Cynthia and Lucinda. Origin: English, American
- Betty, meaning either oath of God, or God is satisfaction. Origin: Greek, American, Hebrew, English

- Caree, meaning manly. Origin: English
- Aldous, German Aldo, an Old German name meaning old. Origin: English
- Kempe, warrior. Origin: English
- Belinda, snake. Origin: German, American, English, Latin, Italian, Spanish
- Byrtel, From the bird hill. Origin: English
- Wacleah, From Wake's meadow. Origin: English
- Emerald, The gemstone emerald. Origin: English, American, Spanish
- Daran, Great. Origin: English, Gaelic
- Alison, Sweet. Origin: German, American, French, English, Irish, Scottish, Teutonic
- Brenton, Hilltop. Origin: Celtic, English, American
- Baldhere, Bold army. Origin: English
- Calinda, Lark. Origin: Greek, Italian, English
- Beornham, From the nobleman's home. Origin: English
- Brayden, Broad hillside. Origin: English, Irish, American
- Smetheleah, From the flat meadow. Origin: English

- Christeena, Follower of Christ. Origin: English, Latin
- Clemento, Gentle. Origin: English
- Katilyn, English abbreviation of Katherine. Pure. Origin: English
- Aethelmaere, Infamous. Origin: English
- D'Arcy, Dark. Origin: Irish, English, French
- Channing, Young wolf. Origin: Irish, American, English, French
- Okes, From the oak. Origin: English
- Boc, Male deer. Origin: English
- Cadi, Pure. Origin: Welsh, English, Irish
- Hand, Worker. Origin: English
- Cartere, Drives a cart. Origin: English
- Brandon, Prince, or brave. Origin: Irish, American, Teutonic, English, Shakespearean
- Carlton, From the land between the streams. Origin: Scottish, American, English
- Beaton, From the warrior's estate. Origin: English
- Bronsonn, Son of a dark man. Origin: English
- Bartholome, Son of a farmer. Origin: English

- Berwynn, Harvest-time friend. Origin: English
- Nichele, Blend of Nichole and Michelle. Origin: English
- Thom, Twin. Origin: Aramaic, English
- Axton, Swordsman's stone. Origin: English
- Janene, Origin: English
- Becky, Abbreviation of Rebecca. Origin: English, American, Hebrew
- Denys, Follower of Dionysius (Greek god of wine). Origin: Greek, English, French
- Leverton, From the rush farm. Origin: English
- Bradlea, Origin: English
- Lawford, From the ford at the hill. Origin: English
- Ilena, Origin: English
- Aylmer, Of awe inspiring fame. Origin: Teutonic, English
- Bede, Name of a historian. Origin: Anglo-Saxon, English
- Darence, Blend of Darell and Clarence. Origin: English
- Fagan, Joyful. Origin: English, Irish
- Birkitt, Area of birch trees. Origin: English

- Osraed, Divine counselor. Origin: English
- Ellyce, Greek form of Elijah. Origin: English
- Beryl, Derived from the precious stone Beryl, a gemstone. Origin: English, American, Greek
- Cecillo, Blind, Origin: English
- Alfie, Wise. Origin: English
- Queena, Queen. Origin: English, Teutonic
- Nik, People's victory. Origin: Greek, English
- Lexandra, Defender of mankind. Feminine of Alexander. Origin: English, Greek
- Bourn, From the brook. Origin: English
- Brione, The name of a flowering vine used in folk medicine. Origin: English, Greek
- Thormond, Thor's protection. Origin: English
- Benjamin, Son of the right hand. Origin: Biblical, American, English, Hebrew
- Marc, Hammer. Origin: Latin, American, English, French
- Hollee, The holly tree. Common name given Christmas girl babies. Origin: English

- Banjiman, Right-hand son. Origin: English
- Charli, Manly. Origin: English
- Valerie, Brave. Origin: French, American, English, Latin
- Xandra, Defender of mankind. Feminine of Alexander. Origin: English, Greek
- Jacqui, Abbreviation of Jacqueline which is the feminine of Jacques. Origin: English, French
- Allaryce, Rules all. Feminine of Alaric. Origin: English, German
- Britney, Origin: English, American
- Leo, Lion. Origin: English, American, Latin, Teutonic
- Marlyssa, Woman from Magdala. Origin: English
- Elyce, Greek form of Elijah. Origin: English
- Dalten, Dale town; valley town. Origin: English
- Burckhardt, Strong castle. Origin: English
- Cingeswiella, Lives at the king's spring. Origin: English
- Jeneva, Phonetic. Origin: English
- Delevan, Friend; good friend. Origin: English

- Denzil, British town. Origin: English, American
- Booker, Bible. Origin: English, American
- Hadley, From the heath covered meadow. Origin: English
- Aiston, From the ash tree farm. Origin: English
- Bolton, From the manor farm. Origin: English
- Odom, Son in law. Origin: English
- Attewell, Lives by the spring. Origin: English
- Berangari, Spearbearer maid. Origin: English
- Fairleigh, Bull meadow. Origin: English
- Augustus, Majestic dignity; grandeur. Origin: German, American, English, Biblical, Latin
- Essie, Star. Origin: Latin, American, Persian, English, French
- Brienna, Strong. Origin: Celtic, English
- Frankie, From France or 'free one.' Feminine of Francis. Origin: Latin, American, English
- Cenehard, Bold guardian. Origin: English
- Cecilia, Blind. Origin: Swedish, American, Latin, English

- Bronnson, Son of a dark man. Origin: English
- Dannelle, Feminine God will judge. Origin: English
- Ellswerth, Great man's home. Origin: English
- Christiaan, Follower of Christ. Origin: English
- Mariah, Bitter. Origin: English, French, American
- Percy, Pierces the valley. Origin: English, American, French
- Kadie, Rhyming, meaning pure. Origin: English
- Brun, Brown or dark. Origin: Anglo-Saxon, English
- Cassandra, Prophetess. Origin: Latin, American, English, Greek, Shakespearean
- Yoman, Retainer. Origin: English
- Hunig, Sweet. Origin: English
- Adkyn, Oaken. Origin: English
- Aeccestane, Swordsman's stone. Origin: English
- Faryn, Adventurous. Origin: English
- Dannia, Feminine God will judge. Origin: English

- Cary, The dark one. Origin: Celtic, American, English
- Raven, Dark haired or wise. Origin: English, American
- Ina, Origin: English, American
- Varek, From the fortress. Origin: English
- Kamlyn, Lord. Origin: Japanese, English
- Grantley, From the large meadow. Origin: English
- Ellis, The Lord is my God. Origin: Hebrew, American, Greek, English
- Ashleen, Meadow of ash trees. Origin: English
- Lawley, From the hill meadow. Origin: English
- Averil, meaning boar-battle. Origin: English, Latin
- Orahamm, From tbe riverbank enclosure. Origin: English
- Janae, God has answered. Origin: English, American
- Galton, From the town on the high ground. Origin: English
- Caster, From the Roman camp. Origin: English
- Bainbrydge, Lives near the bridge over the white water. Origin: English

- Farrs, Son of Farr. Origin: English
- Clemmy, Gentle. Origin: English
- Boone, Good; a blessing. American frontier hero Daniel Boone. Origin: English, French
- Baldur, Prince. Origin: Scandinavian, English, Norse
- Garred, from Gerald 'rules by the spear. Origin: English
- Elwold, Old Welshman. Origin: English
- Brittnee, Origin: English
- Braeden, Broad hillside. Origin: English, Irish, American
- Audri, Nobility; strength. Origin: English
- Guyon, Lively. Origin: English
- Ethelbert, Name of a king. Origin: Anglo-Saxon, English
- Albany, From Albanus meaning 'of Alba. Origin: Latin, English, Scottish, Shakespearean
- Dawnette, The first appearance of daylight; daybreak. Origin: English
- Brady, Spirited. Origin: Gaelic, American, English, Irish
- Daney, From Denmark. Also a feminine God will judge. Origin: English
- Brok, Badger. Origin: English

- Chandler, Candle maker. Origin: English, American, French
- Jonetta, Modern feminine of John and Jon. Origin: English
- Briggs, From the village near a bridge. Origin: English
- LaVyrle, Origin: English
- Rashae, Blend of Ray and Shawn. Origin: English
- Burgaud, Strong castle. Origin: English
- Bliths, Joy. Origin: English
- Beck, Brook. Origin: English, Swedish
- Nikko, Abbreviation of Nicholas. Origin: English, Japanese
- Parnel, Origin: English, Irish
- Nanci, meaning favor; grace. Origin: English, American, French
- Beverleigh, Beaver stream. Origin: English
- Blaecleah, From the dark meadow. Origin: English
- Alhrick, Sacred ruler. Origin: English
- Bradlee, Origin: English
- Radmund, Red haired defender. Origin: English
- Ashlee, Meadow of ash trees. Origin: English, American

- Casey, Brave. Origin: Gaelic, American, Spanish, Irish, Biblical, English, French, Greek, Latin
- Dennison, Dennis' son. Origin: English, Greek
- Aekerley, From the oak tree meadow. Origin: English
- Kammi, Lord. Origin: Japanese, English
- Aswynn, Friend with a spear. Origin: English
- Bessie, meaning either oath of God, or God is satisfaction. Origin: Greek, American, Hebrew, English
- Havyn, Safety. Origin: English
- Aesctun, From the ash tree farm. Origin: English
- Claudius, Lame. Origin: Biblical, English, Latin, Shakespearean
- Bennet, Right-hand son. Origin: English, Latin, French
- Brewster, One who brews ale. See also Webster. Origin: English
- Brionne, The name of a flowering vine used in folk medicine. Origin: English, Greek
- Parkinson, Son of Parkin. Origin: English
- Derell, Open. Origin: English, French
- Chip, Man. Origin: English, American

- Bedford, meaning Bede's ford. Origin: English, American, Shakespearean
- Brettany, Brit. Origin: English, French
- Melynda, Blend of Melissa and Linda. Origin: English, Greek
- Reynold, Strong judgment. Origin: Teutonic, American, English, German, French
- Denly, Meadow by a valley. Origin: English
- Letitia, Happy. Origin: Spanish, American, Latin, English
- Buckie, Male deer. Origin: English, Greek
- Kade, From the wetlands. Origin: Gaelic, Scottish, American
- Botolf, Wolf. Origin: English, German
- Aethelmaer, Noble or famous. Origin: English
- Birdena, Little bird. Origin: English
- Alder, From the alder tree. Origin: English
- Aubriana, Rules with elf-wisdom. Origin: English, French
- Kadienne, Rhyming, meaning pure. Origin: English
- Melvyn, Chief. Origin: Irish, American, Celtic, English

- Birtle, From the bird hill. Origin: English
- Burty, Bright light. Origin: English
- Jerald, Variant and surname form of Gerald: Rules by the spear. Origin: English, American
- Burgard, Strong castle. Origin: English
- Quint, fifth.' Surname. Origin: English, French
- Daly, Gather together. Origin: Irish, English, Gaelic
- Chadburn, From the wildcat brook. Origin: English
- Brandee, beverage brandy used as a given name. Origin: English, American
- Nigel, Dark. Origin: Latin, American, Irish, English, Scandinavian, Gaelic
- Kapri, Caprice. Origin: English
- Erwin, White river. Origin: Welsh, American, English
- Hob, Famed, bright, shining. Origin: German, English
- Clayten, Town by a clay bed. Origin: English
- Belle, Intelligent. Origin: Hungarian, American, English, French, German, Spanish, Latin

- Jonell, Modern feminine of John and Jon. Origin: English
- Cadie, meaning a rhythmic flow of sounds. Origin: English, Irish
- Aeker, From the oak tree. Origin: English
- Jenella, Origin: English
- Niewheall, From the new hall. Origin: English
- Bird, Bird. Origin: English, American
- Elbert, noble. Origin: English, American, German, Teutonic
- Hamnet, House or home. Origin: English, German
- Gail, Lively. Origin: English, American
- Marden, From the valley with the pool. Origin: English
- Jillianne, Jove's child.from the masculine Julian. Origin: English
- Jonay, Modern feminine of John and Jon. Origin: English
- Afreda, Created. Produced. Origin: Muslim, English
- Salford, From the willow ford. Origin: English
- Boy, Boy. Origin: English
- Spalding, From the split meadow. Origin: English

- Kay, Fire. Origin: Scottish, American, Greek, Welsh, Arthurian Legend, English
- Udell, From the yew tree valley. Origin: English
- Carr, Fighter. Origin: Celtic, English, Norse, Scottish
- Eddis, Son of Edward. Origin: English
- Holea, Holy. Origin: English
- Blaeey, Blond. Origin: English
- Radcliffe, Red cliff. Origin: English
- Daine, From Denmark. Origin: English, French
- Ede, Wealthy guardian. Origin: English
- Gilford, From Gill'S ford. Origin: English
- Carlson, free men's town. Origin: English
- Christianos, Follower of Christ. Origin: English
- Weslia, Feminine of Wesley. Origin: English
- Lester, From the Legion's camp. Origin: Latin, American, English
- Udolf, Wealthy wolf. Origin: English
- Alexandrea Feminine of Alexander. Defender of mankind. Origin: English, Greek, American
- China, Place name. Origin: English

- Bertold, Bright light. Origin: English, Teutonic, German
- Shelley, From the ledge meadow. Origin: Anglo-Saxon, English, American
- Lacey, Origin: English, American, French
- Del, Valley. Origin: English, American, French
- Betsy, meaning either oath of God, or God is satisfaction. Origin: Greek, American, Hebrew, English
- Talon, Sharp. Origin: French, American, English
- Liora, sweet bay tree symbolic of honor and victory. Old name with many variants. Origin: English, Latin
- Maed, From the meadow. Origin: English
- Yardley, From the enclosed meadow. Origin: English
- Levyna, Issh. Origin: English
- Zina, Welcoming; hospitable. Origin: English, American
- Nana, Grace. Origin: Hebrew, American, Hawaiian, Spanish
- Blaed, Wealthy glory. Origin: English
- Auberon, Rules with elf-wisdom. Origin: English

- Calder, From the stony river. Origin: Celtic, English, Scottish
- Beadutun, From the warrior's estate. Origin: English
- Sheridan, Bright. Origin: Gaelic, Celtic, Irish, English
- Hertha, Of the earth. Origin: English, German, American, Teutonic
- Cedrych, Origin: English, Welsh
- Cherrell, dear one; darling. Origin: English
- Franki, Modern variants of Frances meaning From France or free one. Origin: English
- Jack, a rebel. Origin: Shakespearean, American, Hebrew, Polish, English
- Aylmar, noble. Origin: English, Teutonic
- Braddford, Broad stream. Origin: English
- Byram, From the cattle yard. Origin: English
- Carl, Man. Origin: English, American, German
- Bo, Precious. Origin: Chinese, English, Scandinavian
- Lawly, From the hill meadow. Origin: English
- Jayni, Jehovah has been gracious; has shown favor. Origin: English

- Brendt, Hilltop. Origin: Celtic, English
- Dontaye, Contemporary phonetic'enduring. Origin: English
- Doreen, Beautiful. Origin: Greek, American, French, Gaelic, Celtic, English, Irish
- Ilse, God is satisfaction. Origin: Hebrew, Greek, English, Teutonic, German
- Albern, Noble warrior. Origin: English, Teutonic
- Berengaria, Spearbearer maid. Origin: English, German
- Claudelle, Feminine of Claude. Origin: English, German
- Nanci, meaning favor; grace. Origin: English, American, French
- Katlynne, Medieval English form of the Irish Caitlin. 'Pure'. Origin: English
- Faine, Good-natured. Origin: English
- Talbot, Henry VI, Part 1' Lord Talbot. Shakespearean, English, French
- Smith, Tradesman. Origin: English, American, Shakespearean
- Ashwin, Spear friend. Origin: English
- Cibil, prophetess or fortune-teller. Origin: English
- Ave, Fighting boar. Origin: English

- Gypsy, Wanderer. Origin: English
- Percival, Destroyer. Origin: Latin, American, Arthurian Legend, English, French
- Dack, Reference to the French town Dax. Origin: English
- Tahurer, Drummer. Origin: English
- Queeny, Queen. Origin: English, Teutonic
- Cleavon, Cliff. Origin: African-American, English
- Cetewind, From the cottage on the winding path. Origin: English
- Sheldon, From the hill on the ledge. Origin: Anglo-Saxon, American, English
- Hawly, From the hedged meadow. Origin: English
- Fayanna, Confidence; trust; belief. Origin: English, French
- Olita, Winged. Origin: English
- Dael, Small valley. Origin: Dutch, English
- Danforth, Place name in Britain. Origin: English
- Britton, Brit. A native of Brittany. Origin: English, American
- Hammond, House or home. Introduced from Germany during the Norman

Conquest. Also used as a surname. Origin: English, German

- Melvin, Chief. Origin: Irish, American, Celtic, English
- Burghere, Lives at the fortress. Origin: English
- Elynn, Means light or most beautiful woman. Origin: English
- Daelyn, Small valley. Origin: English
- Ellesse, Abbreviation of Eleanor and Ellen. Origin: English
- Litton, From tbe hillside town. Origin: English
- Melvina, Handmaiden. Origin: Celtic, American, Gaelic, English
- Oakden, From the oak tree valley. Origin: English
- Isham, From the iron one's estate. Origin: English, American
- Ulger, Wolf spear. Origin: English
- Chann, Young wolf. Origin: English, Irish
- Dacian, Of the nobility. Origin: English, French, Gaelic, Latin
- Nancie, Favor; grace. Origin: English
- Wenda, Comely. Origin: English, German, Teutonic

- Adamson, Son of Adam. Origin: English, Hebrew
- Perceval, Hero of several Arthurian stories. Origin: Arthurian Legend, English, French
- Botulf, Wolf. Origin: English, German
- Allard, Resolute. Origin: Teutonic, English, French
- Cleva, Dwells at the cliffs. Origin: English
- Alhraed, Divine counselor. Origin: English
- Carolanne, Feminine manly. Origin: English
- Darek, Gifted ruler. From Theodoric. Origin: English, German
- Burt, Origin: English, American
- Fayanna, Confidence; trust; belief. Origin: English, French
- Franky, Frenchman. Origin: Latin, English, French
- Melody, Melody. Origin: English, American, Greek
- Davis, David's son. Origin: English, Scottish, American
- Kamrin, Modernused for girls. Origin: English
- Atteworthe, Lives at the farmstead. Origin: English

- Radburn, Lives by the red stream. Origin: English
- Phil, Fond of horses. Form of Phillip. Origin: English, American, Greek
- Janet, Gift from God. Origin: Hebrew, American, English, Scottish
- Boston, A place name. Origin: English, American
- Kaci, vigorus. Origin: English, American
- Brentin, Mountain peak. Origin: English
- Iva, Gift from God. Origin: Hebrew, American, English, French
- Blaire, Flatland. Origin: English, Scottish
- Kaden, Companion. Origin: Arabic, American
- Birche, Birch. Origin: English
- Eadwiella From the old spring. Origin: English
- Cheston, Camp. Origin: English
- Audreana, Nobility; strength. Origin: English
- Clark, Derived from a surname meaning cleric or clerk. Origin: English, American
- Ricadene, Lives in the ruler. Origin: English

- Brooke, Water; stream. Actress Brooke Shields. Origin: English, American
- Jenay, meaning 'God has answered. '. Origin: English
- Hadden, From the heath. Origin: English
- Davinia, Cherished. Origin: Hebrew, Scottish, English
- Wes, West meadow.English surname Westley. Origin: English, American
- York, From the bear estate. Origin: English, Celtic, Shakespearean
- Jonni, Modern feminine of John and Jon. Origin: English
- Faye, Confidence; trust; belief. Origin: English, American, French
- Bretta, From Britain. Origin: Celtic, English, French
- Garrison, Spear-fortified town. Origin: English, German, American
- Ogdon, From the oak tree valley. Origin: English
- Cenewyg, Bold warrior. Origin: English
- Cenewig, Bold warrior. Origin: English
- Waefreleah, From the quaking aspen tree meadow. Origin: English
- Hughette, Little Hugh. Origin: English
- Haesel, Nut. Origin: English

- Alano, Handsome. Origin: Spanish, English
- Kaci, vigorous. Origin: English, American
- Fay, Fairy. Also a, meaning: Confidence; trust; belief. Origin: French, American, English
- Bina, Origin: English
- Albie, Old English for brilliant; bright. Origin: English
- Ashlyn, Meadow of ash trees. Origin: English, American
- Charlotte, Feminine manly. Origin: English, American, French
- Beornet, Leader. Origin: English
- Katlynn, Medieval English form of the Irish Caitlin. Pure. Origin: English, American
- Attley, From the meadow. Origin: English
- Brianne, Strong. Origin: Irish, American, Celtic, English
- Atwood, Lives in the forest. Origin: English
- Alita, Origin: Spanish, English, French
- Thornly, From the thorny meadow. Origin: English
- Gilda, Serves God. Origin: Celtic, American, English

- Jerad, rules by the spear. Origin: English, American, Hebrew
- Caddarik, Battle leader. Origin: English
- Gail, father's joy. Origin: Hebrew, American, English
- Claude, Lame. Origin: English, American, French, Latin
- Dariel, Open. Origin: English, French
- Ashlynne, Meadow of ash trees. Origin: English
- Cara, Friend. Origin: Celtic, American, English, Italian, Latin
- Jerel, Strong; open-minded. Blend of Jerold and Darell. Origin: English, American
- Carol, meaning strong or manly. Origin: English, American, French
- Allan, Fair; handsome. Also both a (noble, bright) and an abbreviation of names beginning with Al-. Origin: English, American, Celtic
- Nykko, Abbreviation of Nicholas. Origin: English
- Christy, Christian. Origin: Scottish, English
- Burgess, Lives in town. Origin: English, Celtic

- Barthelmy, Son of a farmer. Both surname and given name. Origin: English
- Bartholomieu, Son of a farmer. Origin: English
- Aegelmaere, Infamous. Origin: English
- Hillocke, From the small hill. Origin: English
- Fraze, French town. Origin: English
- Berk, The birch tree meadow. Also see Barclay and Burke. Origin: English, Irish, French, Turkish
- Jenetta, Origin: English
- Bardou, Bright wolf, ax-wielding wolf. Origin: English
- Carter, Cart driver, cart maker. Origin: English, American
- Templeton, Temple-town. Origin: English
- Bessy, meaning either oath of God, or God is satisfaction. Origin: Greek, Hebrew, English
- Ace, Unity. Origin: Anglo-Saxon, American, English, Latin
- Branddun, From the beacon hill. Origin: English
- Ashly, Meadow of ash trees. Origin: English, American

- Dalenna, Small valley. Abbreviation of Madeline. Origin: English
- Bradleigh, Origin: English
- Chadbyrne, From the wildcat brook. Origin: English
- Uldwyna, Special friend. Origin: English
- Janee, Jehovah has been gracious; has shown favor. Origin: English, Hebrew
- Kandiss, Modern- ancient hereditary title used by Ethiopian queens. Origin: English
- Bick, From the hewer's ford. Origin: English
- Irvin, White. Origin: Celtic, American, Scottish, English
- Deona, Divine. Origin: English
- Kaeleigh, keeper of the keys; pure. Origin: English
- Burleigh, Lives at the castle's meadow. Fortified. See also Berlyn. Origin: English, Teutonic
- Blanford, Gray man's ford; gray haired. Origin: English
- Smyth, Tradesman. Origin: English
- Attwell, Lives by the spring. Origin: English
- Birlie, Cow pasture. Origin: English

- Mabella, Beautiful and loving. Origin: Latin, English
- Somerton, From the summer estate. Origin: English
- Fawn, Young deer. Origin: English, American
- Gibson, Gilbert's Son. Origin: English
- Eadelmarr, noble. Origin: English
- Camden, From the winding valley. Origin: Anglo-Saxon, Scottish, American, English, Gaelic
- Britani, Origin: English
- Ashleah, Meadow of ash trees. Origin: English
- Dorinda, meaning Gift of God. Origin: English, American, Greek
- Berford, From the barley ford. Origin: English
- Brookson, Son of Brooke. Origin: English
- Aylwin, Friend. Origin: German, English, Teutonic
- Brittaney, Origin: English, American
- Heywood, From the hedged forest. Origin: English
- Barrington, Fair-haired. Origin: Irish, English

- Caldwell, From the cold spring. Origin: English
- Tedmond, National protector. Origin: English
- Marigold, Marigold (flower name). Origin: English
- Ember, Hot ashes. Origin: English
- Yul Born at Christmas. Origin: English
- Charly, a man. Origin: English
- Hid, From the hide. Origin: English
- Augusta, Origin: English, American, Latin
- Austin, Origin: French, American, Latin, English
- Cal, Bald, Origin: English, American
- Barkley, Birch valley; birch tree meadow. Origin: English
- Garroway, Spear fighter. Origin: English
- D'Arcy, Origin: English, French
- Gibbesone, Gilbert's Son. Origin: English
- Daisy, The day's eye. Origin: Anglo-Saxon, American, English
- Claiborn, From the clay brook. Origin: English
- Welss, From the west. Origin: English
- Autumn, Born in the fall; The fall season. Origin: English, American
- Janette, Gift from God. Origin: Hebrew, American, English

- Jerett, Spear strong. Origin: English
- Eldan, From the elves'valley. Origin: English
- Gijs, Bright. Origin: English
- Birdhil, From the bird hill. Origin: English
- Marshall, Horse servant; marshal; steward. Origin: French, American, English
- Billy, Nickname for William 'resolute protector'. Origin: English, American, German
- Burly, Lives at the castle's meadow. Origin: English
- Osburn, Divine warrior. Origin: English
- Quent, fifth.' Surname. Origin: English, French
- Rae, Doe. Origin: English, Scandinavian, American, Hebrew
- Thompson, Derives from Thomas 'Twin. Origin: English
- Bax, Baker. Origin: English
- Oliver, Affectionate. Origin: Norse, American, Shakespearean, English, French, German, Latin
- Celdtun, From the farm by the spring. Origin: English
- Baillie, Steward; bailiff. Origin: English

- Kendall, From the bright valley. Origin: Celtic, American, English
- Dee, Origin: English, American
- Leontyne, Lioness. Origin: Latin, English
- Olexa, Defender of mankind. Feminine of Alexander. Origin: English, Greek, Czechoslovakian
- Dawnelle, The first appearance of daylight; daybreak. Origin: English
- Dacey, Of the nobility. Origin: English, French, Gaelic
- Cingeswell, Lives at the king's spring. Origin: English
- Osmar, Divinely glorious. Origin: English
- Carmel, Garden. Origin: English, Hebrew, Biblical
- Osmond, God's protection. Origin: Teutonic, Scandinavian, English
- Ivie, A climbing evergreen ornamental plant. Origin: English
- Rexlord, From the king's ford. Origin: English
- Gehard, Spear hard. Origin: English
- Wacian, Watchful. Origin: Anglo-Saxon, English
- Letitia, name Letitia. 'Joyful;happy. Origin: English

- Adair, From the ford by the oak trees. Origin: Celtic, English, Gaelic, Scottish
- Davina, Cherished. Origin: Hebrew, American, English, Scottish
- Briann, Strong. She ascends. Feminine of Brian. Origin: Celtic, English
- August, Origin: English, American, German, Latin
- Aethelweard, Noble protector. Origin: English
- Garrard, Brave with a spear. Origin: English
- Bayley, Courtyard within castle walls. Origin: English, French
- Jacy, Based on the initials J. C. or an abbreviation of Jacinda. Origin: English
- Chresta, Follower of Christ. Origin: English
- Wendi, Origin: English, American
- Alexi, Helper, defender of man. Origin: English, Greek
- Cai, Arthur's brother. Origin: Arthurian Legend, English, Welsh
- Gaila, Joyful. Origin: English
- Aiwyn, Wise friend. Origin: English

- Carlatun, From Carl's farm. Origin: English
- Herve, warrior. Origin: Teutonic, English
- Nedra, Feminine of Ned. Origin: English, American
- Audley, Old friend. Origin: English, Anglo-Saxon
- Dawnetta, The first appearance of daylight; daybreak. Origin: English
- Milbyrne, From the mill stream. Origin: English
- Austina, Origin: English, French, Latin
- Ashlen, Meadow of ash trees. Origin: English
- Austen, Origin: French, American, English
- Haestingas, Violent. Origin: English
- Austyn, Origin: French, American, English
- Rapere, Maker of rope. Origin: English
- Baily, Steward; bailiff. Origin: English
- Cathi, pure. Origin: English
- Darby, without envy. Origin: English, American, Gaelic, Irish, Norse
- Hallwell, Lives by the holy spring. Origin: English
- Alida, noble. Origin: Dutch, American, English, German, Latin

- Catrice, Modern blend of Catrina and Patrice. Origin: English
- Charles, Manly. Origin: French, Teutonic, American, English, German, Shakespearean
- Blair, From tbe plain. Origin: Celtic, American, English, Gaelic, Irish, Scottish
- Janaya, God has answered. Origin: English
- Jimmy, Supplanter. Origin: Hebrew, American, English
- Beth, meaning either oath of God, or God is satisfaction. Origin: Greek, American, Aramaic, English, Hebrew, Scottish
- Cecilie, Blind. Origin: Latin, English
- Austyn, Origin: French, American, English
- Adrian, Black; dark; of the Adriatic. Origin: Latin, American, English, Shakespearean
- Jaci, or an abbreviation of Jacinda. Origin: English
- Isenham, From the iron one's estate. Origin: English

- Hodsone, Son of the hooded man. Origin: English
- Barbi, Traveler from a foreign land. Origin: English, Greek
- Cath, Pure, clear. Origin: French, Latin, English, Irish, Welsh
- Chester, Camp. Origin: Latin, American, English
- Bensen, Ben's son. surname. Origin: English
- Pete, Stone; rock. Origin: Greek, American, English
- Alex, Defender of men; protector of mankind. Origin: Greek, American, English
- George, Origin: Shakespearean, American, English, Greek
- Jacklynn, the feminine of Jacques. Origin: English
- Nancie, meaning favor; grace. Origin: English, American, French
- Dannon, Feminine God will judge. Origin: English
- Ulmar, Wolf famous. Origin: English
- Indee, The country India. Origin: English
- Genna, White wave. Origin: English
- Brawley, From the hillslope meadow. Origin: English

- Branden, Beacon on the hill' or 'gorse-covered hill. Origin: English, American
- Saewald, Sea powerful. Origin: English
- Alberic, Rules with elf-wisdom. Origin: English, Teutonic
- Byrnes, Son of Byrne. Origin: English
- Atkinson, Son of Aiken. Origin: English
- Berresford, Barley field. Origin: English
- Danelle, God is my judge. Origin: Hebrew, American, English
- Aisford, Lives by the ash tree ford. Origin: English
- Parle, Little rock. Origin: English
- Marilynn, Blend of Marie or Mary and Lyn. Origin: English
- Borden, From the boar valley. Origin: Anglo-Saxon, English
- Austin, Origin: French, American, Latin, English
- Jer, Origin: English
- Bazil, Royal; kingly. Origin: English
- Laibrook, Lives by the path by the brook. Origin: English
- Aldora, noble. Origin: English, Greek

- Macie, Derived from medieval male form of Matthew. Origin: English, American
- Esmond, Protected by God. Origin: English
- Aundre, Manly; brave. Modern. Origin: English
- Joana, Origin: English, Latin, American
- Danya, God is my judge. Origin: Hebrew, English
- Graent, Great. Origin: English
- Bardo, Origin: Danish, Aramaic, English
- Danitza, Feminine God will judge. Origin: English
- Chadwick, Protector; defender. Origin: English, American
- Blandford, Gray man's ford; gray haired. Origin: English
- Wadley, From Wade's meadow. Origin: English
- Sherman, Cuts the nap of woolen cloth. Origin: English, American, German
- Fauna, Fawn. Origin: French, Latin, English
- Addaneye, Lives on the noble's island. Origin: English
- Kailyn, pure. Origin: English, American

- Wells, Lives by the spring. Origin: English
- Marisa, Origin: English, Latin, American, Spanish, Hebrew
- Birney, Lives on the brook island. Origin: English
- Buddey, Friend. Origin: English
- Georgie, tiller of the soil, or farmer. Origin: English
- Avelyn, given names Aveline and Avis. Origin: English
- Allin, Fair; handsome. Also both a (noble, bright) and an abbreviation of names beginning with Al-. Origin: English
- Halton, From the hillslope estate. Origin: English
- Cicero, Chickpea. Origin: Latin, American, English, Shakespearean
- Dannell, Feminine God will judge. Origin: English
- Attewode, Lives in the forest. Origin: English
- Beamer, Trumpeter. Origin: English
- Val, Strong. Origin: English, American, Latin, Persian

- Bart, From the barley farm. Origin: English, American, Hebrew
- Dennie, Origin: English, Greek, American
- Bartley, Ploughman. Origin: Aramaic, Hebrew, English, Scottish
- Nye, Origin: Welsh, English
- Bishop, Bishop; overseer. Origin: English, American
- Davita, Beloved. Feminine of David. Origin: English
- Jeraldine, Origin: English, American
- Bryana, Strong. She ascends. Feminine of Brian. Origin: Celtic, American, English
- Bassett, Short. Origin: English
- Marchman, From the march. Origin: English
- Haele, Lives in the hall. Origin: English
- Alden, Defender. Origin: Anglo-Saxon, American, English
- Blossom, Fresh. Origin: English, American
- Banjamen, Right-hand son. Origin: English
- Carlotta, Manly. Origin: Spanish, American, English, French, Italian
- Clerc, Scholar. Origin: English

- Mardon, From the valley with the pool. Origin: English
- Beldin, Beautiful vale/valley. Origin: English
- Hunt, Pursuer. Origin: English
- Aubry, Rules with elf-wisdom. Origin: English, French
- Ulric, Wolf ruler. Origin: English, Teutonic
- Aldan, From the old manor. Origin: English
- Beorhttun, From the fortified town. Origin: English
- Southwell, From the south spring. Origin: English, Shakespearean
- Vance, Marshland. Origin: English, American
- Fulbert, meaning very bright. Origin: English
- Jenarae, Origin: English
- Benny, Right-hand son. Origin: English, American, Latin, Hebrew
- Zelma, Comely. Origin: English, American
- Brinton, From Brinton. Origin: English
- Blondell, Fair-haired. Origin: English, French

- Milly, Servant for the temple. Origin: Latin, English, German
- Hadwyn, War friend. Origin: English, Teutonic
- Blade, Wealthy glory. Origin: English
- Ellmer, noble. Origin: English
- Genny, White wave. Origin: English
- Kaedee, Rhymingor Cady. Origin: English
- Cadabyr, From the warrior's settlement. Origin: English
- Waed, Advancer. Origin: English
- Harvey, warrior. Origin: Teutonic, American, Celtic, German, English, French
- Cecil, Blind, Origin: English, American, Latin
- Faulkner, Falconer; one who trains falcons. Origin: English
- Pernell, Little rock. Origin: English, American
- Devry, Derived from place-name Deverel. Origin: English, French
- Bardulph, Bright wolf, ax-wielding wolf. Origin: English
- Bainbridge, Lives near the bridge over the white water. Origin: English, Gaelic
- Madre, Mother. Origin: English, Spanish

- Terence, Smooth. Origin: Latin, American, English, Irish, Norse
- Blakeley, From the light meadow; from the dark meadow. Origin: English
- Ashley, Dwells at the ash tree meadow. Origin: Anglo-Saxon, American, English
- Bronsin, Son of a dark man. Origin: English
- Benon, Industrious. Origin: English
- Gaylen, Festive party. Origin: English
- Grantland, From the large meadow. Origin: English
- Branwel, Place name in Britain. Origin: English
- Alao, Fair; handsome. Also both a (noble, bright) and an abbreviation of names beginning with Al-. Origin: English
- Holdin, From the hollow in the valley. Origin: English
- Daelan, Rhyming- a historical blacksmith with supernatural powers. Origin: English
- Eibhear, Strong as a boar. Origin: English

- Niko, Abbreviation of Nicholas. Origin: English, American
- Neda, Born on Sunday. Origin: Slavic, English
- Saebeorht, Glory at sea. Origin: English
- Emblyn, meaning labor. Origin: English, French
- Arvon, The people's friend. Origin: English
- Danylynn, Dearly loved. Origin: English
- Fairlee, Bull meadow. Origin: English
- Nikki, Of the Lord. Origin: Latin, English, Japanese
- Idal, From the yew tree valley. Origin: English
- Madelene, From the tower. Origin: Hebrew, English
- Aelfric, Elf ruler. Origin: English
- Birkee, Birch island. Origin: English
- Burkitt, Area of birch trees. Origin: English
- Bryon, Brave. Origin: Celtic, American, English
- Carlisle, From the protected tower. Origin: English, Shakespearean
- Carvell, From the villa by the march. Origin: English, French

- Rashaun, Blend of Ray and Shawn. Origin: English
- Garrman, Speannan. Origin: English
- Arwood, From the fir forest. Origin: English
- Barrclay, Birch valley; birch tree meadow. Origin: English
- Gill, Young. Origin: Latin, English
- Ashlin, Meadow of ash trees. Origin: English
- Bobbie, Origin: English, American
- Albert, Intelligent or noble. Origin: German, American, Hungarian, English, Swedish, Teutonic
- Ike, Isaac 'Laughter. Origin: English, American, Hebrew
- Brighton, Place name in Britain. Origin: English
- Radley, From the red meadow. Origin: English
- Atheistan, Origin: English
- Chynna, Based on the country name China. Origin: English
- Blayke, Light; dark. Origin: English
- Dany, Feminine God will judge. Origin: English

- Derick, Gifted ruler. From Theodoric. Origin: English, German, American
- Cilla, Origin: English, Latin
- Maegth, Maiden. Origin: English
- Aland, Fair; handsome. Also both a (noble, bright) and an abbreviation of names beginning with Al-. Origin: English
- Bill, Nickname for William 'resolute protector'. Origin: English, American, German
- Athemar, Noble or famous. Origin: English
- Elberte, Noble or glorious. Origin: English
- Brandi, beverage brandy used as a given name. Origin: English, American, Italian
- Milo, Merciful. Origin: English, German, American, Greek
- Laci, Origin: English, American, French
- Alfrid, Sage. Origin: English
- Gussie, Majestic, grand. Origin: Latin, American, Greek, English
- Esmund, Protected by God. Origin: English
- Bardan, Lives near the boar's den. Origin: English
- Hugiet, Little Hugh. Origin: English

- Babs, foreign or strange, Origin: English
- Derik, Gifted ruler. From Theodoric. Origin: English, German, American
- Oakes, From the oak. Origin: English
- Kayci, Modern Kacie, Origin: English
- Atkinsone, Son of Aiken. Origin: English
- Claeg, Mortal. Origin: English
- Cidney, Origin: English
- Marsha, Origin: English, American, Latin
- Galea, Festive party. Origin: English
- Bletsung, Consecrated. Origin: English
- Benjaman, Right-hand son. Origin: English, American
- Theyn, Follower. Origin: English
- Hastings, Violent. Origin: English, Shakespearean
- Bickford, From the hewer's ford. Origin: English
- Bud, Origin: English, American
- Mary, Wished-for child, rebellion and bitter. Origin: Hebrew, American, Biblical, English
- Carnell, Defender of the castle. Origin: English, American
- Carver, Carves wood or sculpts. Origin: English

- Calynda, Lark. Origin: Greek, Italian, English
- Zaine or John. Origin: English
- Benejamen, Right-hand son. Origin: English
- Alexia, Defender of men, helper. Greek, American, English
- Burhtun, From the fortified town. Origin: English
- Basil, Royal. Kingly. Origin: Greek, American, English
- Teela, The bird teal; also the blue-green color. Origin: English
- Jacee, an abbreviation of Jacinda. Origin: English
- Barron, Noble fighter. Origin: Teutonic, American, English
- Lace, Origin: English, French
- Rangley, From the raven's meadow. Origin: English
- Osmont, Divine protector. Origin: English
- Sherburne, From the clear brook. Origin: English
- Bordon, Boar's home. Origin: English
- Davy, Beloved. Feminine of David. Origin: English
- Eadwardsone, Son of Edward. Origin: English

- Byron, From the cottage. Origin: French, Teutonic, American, English
- Alisse, Origin: English
- Barry, Spear. Origin: Gaelic, American, English, Celtic, French, Irish
- Gilburt, Oath. Origin: Teutonic, English
- Blagdon, From the dark valley. Origin: English
- Ollaneg, From Olney. Origin: English
- Aelfthryth, meaning elf, and thryth, meaning strength. Origin: English
- Jacelyn, an abbreviation of Jacinda. Origin: English
- Safford, From the willow ford. Origin: English
- Denzell, a place in Cornwall. Origin: English
- Ashley, Origin: English, American
- Ainsley, Derived from the Brittish Nottinghamshire. Origin: English
- Teige, Good-looking. Origin: English, Irish
- Cadby, From the warrior's settlement. Origin: English, Norse
- Cirilla, Mistress; lady. Feminine of Cyril. Origin: English
- Gherardo, Spear hard. Origin: English

- Maelwine, Strong friend. Origin: English
- Bardawulf, Ax wolf. Origin: English
- Jazlyn, Modern; combination of Jocelyn and the musical term jazz. Origin: English, American
- Dekel, Dusty one; servant. Origin: English, Greek, Arabic
- Slaed, From the valley. Origin: English
- Perkin, Little rock. Origin: English
- Sal, Princess. Origin: Hebrew, English
- Jeren, Modern Jaron 'cry of rejoicing. Origin: English
- Holman, Man from the valley. Origin: English, Teutonic
- Humph, A compound of the words peace and giant. Origin: English
- Eadweard, Wealthy guardian. Origin: English
- Yates, Lives by the gates. Origin: English
- Osman, Godly protection. Origin: English, Scandinavian
- Ashlea, Ash tree meadow. Origin: English
- Hamish, Supplant. Replace.derived from the latin Jacomus. Origin: English, Scottish
- Shermon, meaning 'shireman' or 'shearman. Origin: English, German

- Burhleag, Lives at the castle's meadow. Origin: English
- Kacy, vigorous. Origin: English, American
- Jilly, Abbreviation of Jillian or Gillian. Jove's child. Origin: English
- Ogelsby, Fearsome. Origin: English
- Buddie, Friend. Origin: English, American
- Melvon, Meaning uncertain but possibly 'friend of Michael. Origin: English
- Bonnie, Beautiful. Origin: Latin, American, English, French, Scottish
- Kai, Fire. Origin: Scottish, American, Hawaiian, Welsh
- Garrett, Defender. Origin: Norse, American, Teutonic, Anglo-Saxon, English
- Denzel, A place-name in Cornwall. Origin: English, American
- Edgard, Lucky spearman. Origin: Anglo-Saxon, English, French
- Franki, Free land-owner. Origin: English
- Bartolo, Ploughman. Origin: Spanish, English
- Claegtun, Mortal. Origin: English
- Onslowe, From the zealous one's hill. Origin: English

- Madge, Child of light. Origin: Persian, American, English, Greek
- Audrielle, Nobility; strength. Origin: English
- Jenavieve. Phonetic. Origin: English
- Clay, Mortal. Origin: Teutonic, American, English
- Attmore, From the moor. Origin: English
- Beecher, Lives by the beech tree. Origin: English
- Bain, Bridge. Origin: English, Gaelic
- Brodrik, From the broad ridge. Origin: English
- Jayvee, Phonetic name based on initials. Origin: English
- Fain, Joyful. Origin: English
- Origin: English
- Ainsley, Derived from the Brittish Nottinghamshire. Origin: English, American
- Elyza, My God is bountiful. Origin: English
- Millen, One who grinds grain. Origin: English
- Cedrica, Modern feminine of Cedric. Origin: English
- Bondon, Man of the land. Origin: English

- Jonnie, gracious; has shown favor. Origin: English, French, American
- Radcliff, From the red cliff. Origin: English
- Tedrick, Abbreviation of Theodore. Origin: English, German
- Claefer, Clover. Origin: English
- Osmund, God's protection. Origin: Teutonic, Scandinavian, English
- Dane, Brook. Origin: English, American, Danish, Norse, Scandinavian, Hebrew
- Radclyf, From the red cliff. Origin: English
- Edelmarr, noble. Origin: English
- Jolleen, Origin: English
- Kandice, Modern- ancient hereditary title used by Ethiopian queens. Origin: English, American
- Audria, Nobility; strength. Origin: English
- Cadena, Rhythmic. Origin: English
- Calbex, Shepherd. Origin: English
- Clarence, meaning bright or clear. Famous bearers: George, Duke of... Origin: English, American, Latin, Shakespearean
- Aldrin, Old and wise ruler. Origin: English

- Cadda, Warring. Origin: English
- Butcher, Butcher. Origin: English
- Tammy, A feminine name beginning with 'Tam-'. Origin: English, American
- Marsh, Steward. Origin: French, English
- Wesley, Origin: English, American
- Nara, Happy. Origin: Gaelic, Celtic, English, Native American
- Wendell, Wanderer. Origin: Teutonic, American, English, German
- Irvyn, White. Origin: Celtic, English
- Albin, White. Origin: Polish, American, English, Latin
- Lisabet, Abbreviation of Elizabeth. Origin: English
- Reynald, Counselor-ruler. Origin: English, German
- Laurentia, honor and victory. Origin: English, Latin
- Zain, Origin: English, American, Muslim
- Saelig, From the happy meadow. Origin: English
- Rashane, Blend of Ray and Shawn. Origin: English
- Byrne, From the brook. Origin: English
- Addis, Son of Adam. Origin: English, Hebrew

- Ken, Clear water. Origin: Welsh, American, English, Japanese, Scottish
- Ladbroc, Lives by the path by the brook. Origin: English
- Deena, meaning divine. Origin: English, American
- Belldon, Beautiful vale/valley. Origin: English
- Perye, From the pear tree. Origin: English
- Iona, Violet. Origin: English, American, Celtic, Greek, Scottish
- Mable, Lovable. Origin: English, American, Latin
- Pansy, Flower. Origin: French, Greek, American, English
- Grangere, Farmer. Origin: English
- Eda, Wealthy guardian. Origin: Czechoslovakian, English
- Aldwin, From Ealdwine meaning old friend. Origin: English
- Hadon, From the heath. Origin: English
- Pamela, Name invented for a heroine of the book 'Arcadia'. Origin: English, American, Greek, Latin
- Aliceson, Son of All. Origin: English

- Elbertine, Noble or glorious. Origin: English
- Grant, Great. Origin: Latin, American, English, Scottish
- Lacene, Origin: English, French
- Boyce, Lives near the wood. Origin: English, American, French, Teutonic
- Blaike, Light; dark. Origin: English
- Benssen, Ben's son. surname. Origin: English
- Albertina, Origin: French, American, Teutonic, German, English
- Reyhurn, From the deer's stream. Origin: English
- Bentleah, From the bent grass meadow. Origin: English
- Tamtun, From the quiet river farm. Origin: English
- Cartland, From the land between the streams. Origin: English
- Eferleah, From Ever's meadow. Origin: English
- Brandie, beverage brandy used as a given name. Origin: English, American
- Rexley, From the king's meadow. Origin: English
- Irvetta, Friend of the sea. Origin: English

- Chelsi, a London district. Origin: English, American
- Jonnelle, Modern feminine of John and Jon. Origin: English
- Bellamie, Good-looking companion. Origin: English
- Clemente, Merciful. Origin: Latin, English
- Farris, Rock. Origin: Greek, American, English
- Faithe, Faithful. Origin: English
- Bram, Origin: Irish, Hebrew, Dutch, English, Scottish, Gaelic
- Alanson, Fair; handsome. Also both a (noble, bright) and an abbreviation of names beginning with Al-. Origin: English, Celtic
- Ivey, A climbing evergreen ornamental plant. Ivy. Origin: English
- Haethowine, War friend. Origin: English
- Laurena, Origin: English
- Castle, Castle. Origin: English
- Farson, Son of Farr. Origin: English
- Kendal, Royal valley, referring to Kent in England. Origin: English, American
- Radeliffe, From the red cliff. Origin: English

- Nanette, Grace. Origin: Hebrew, American, French, English
- Blessing, Consecrated. Origin: English
- Charleston, A man. Origin: English
- Peterson, A rock. Form of Peter. Origin: English
- Kendale, Royal valley. Surname referring to Kent in England. Origin: English
- Lacie, Origin: English, American, French
- Kelven, River man. Origin: Celtic, English
- Baynbridge, Bridge. Origin: English
- Clarke, Cleric; secretary. Origin: English
- Claudette, Feminine of Claude. Origin: English, German, American, French
- Jazmina, Modern; combination of Jocelyn and the musical term jazz. Origin: English
- Danvin, Friend. Origin: English
- Burford, Lives at the castle ford. Origin: English
- Jerande, rules by the spear. Origin: English
- Erwyn, White river. Origin: Welsh, English
- Haefen, Safety. Origin: English
- Lad, Attendant. Origin: English

- Bertrand, Shining raven. Origin: Teutonic, American, French, German, English
- Benton, Settlement in a grassy place. Origin: English, American
- Richman, Powerful. Origin: English
- Mareesa, Origin: English, Latin
- Case, Observant; alert; vigorous. Origin: Irish, English
- Marvin, Mariner. Origin: Teutonic, American, English, Celtic, Welsh
- Mercer, Merchant. Origin: English, French, Latin
- Bert, Bright light. Origin: English, American, French, German, Teutonic
- Berry, Flower; berry. Origin: English, American
- Osrick, Divine ruler. Origin: English
- Donte, Contemporary phonetic'enduring. Origin: English, American, Latin
- Bridgely, From the meadow near the bridge. Origin: English
- Braddock, Broad-spreading oak. Origin: English
- Barcley, Birch valley; birch tree meadow. Origin: English

- Gildas, Name of a historian. Origin: Anglo-Saxon, Celtic, English
- Lisabeth, Abbreviation of Elizabeth. Origin: English
- Cabe, Ropemaker. Origin: English
- Hild, noble. Origin: English
- Baxter, Baker. Origin: English, American
- Ceastun, Camp. Origin: English
- Hamelstun, From the grassy estate. Origin: English
- Brioni, The name of a flowering vine used in folk medicine. Origin: English, Greek
- Kamren, Modernused for girls. Origin: English
- Calvino, Bald. Origin: Italian, Spanish, English
- Carson, Surname. Origin: Scottish, American, English
- Chelsee, a London district. Origin: English
- Devyn, Servant. Origin: Gaelic, American, Celtic, Irish, English, Anglo-Saxon
- Cater, One who caters. Origin: English
- Bartel, Ploughman. Origin: Aramaic, Hebrew, English
- Blysse, Joy. Cheer. Origin: English

- Theomund, Wealthy defender. Origin: Anglo-Saxon, Teutonic, English
- Barbara, meaning foreign or strange. Origin: English, American, Greek
- Christana, Follower of Christ. Origin: English
- Clemmons, Gentle. Origin: English
- Jaydee, Phonetic name based on initials. Origin: English
- Athilda, At the elder tree. Origin: English
- Derek, Gifted ruler. From Theodoric. Origin: German, American, Teutonic, English
- Audreanna, Nobility; strength. Origin: English
- Inda, The country India. Origin: English
- Eferhilda, Bear or warrior maiden. Origin: English
- Aescwine, Spear friend. Origin: English
- Blakey, Blond. Origin: English
- Aiken, Oaken. Origin: Anglo-Saxon, English
- Tab, Brilliant. Origin: German, American, English, Hebrew
- Boothe, Lives in a hut. Origin: English
- Immy, Innocent. Origin: English

- Bradwell, From the broad spring. Origin: English
- Carilyn, Feminine manly. Origin: English
- Cherry, Dear one; darling. Origin: French, American, English
- Sagar, Wise one. Surname. Origin: English
- Cedric, Chief. Origin: Celtic, American, English, Welsh
- Cassie, Origin: English, American, Greek
- Barric, Grain farm. Origin: English
- Calvex, Shepherd. Origin: English Calvin, Bald. Origin: English, American, Latin
- Aaric, rule with mercy. Origin: English, Norse
- Isabel, Devoted to God. Origin: Hebrew, American, Spanish, English, Latin, Shakespearean
- Alfred, Name of a king. Origin: Anglo-Saxon, American, Swedish, English, Teutonic
- Basile, royal. Origin: Greek, English
- Oscar, Divine spear. Origin: Norse, American, Celtic, English
- Aleda, Winged. Origin: English, German

- Fay, Fairy. Also a, meaning: Confidence; trust; belief. Origin: French, American, English
- Cayle, Bold. Origin: English
- Elam, Place name in Britain. Origin: English, Biblical, Hebrew
- Garrey, Spear. Origin: English, German
- Adia, Wealthy. Origin: English
- Audrie, Nobility; strength. Origin: English
- Gervase, Servant spear. Origin: Celtic, English
- Norwel, From the north spring. Origin: English
- Berta, Intelligent. Origin: German, Swedish, American, Hungarian, Celtic, Czechoslovakian, Spanish, Teutonic,English
- Beldon, Lives in the beautiful glen. Origin: English
- Beortbtraed, Bright counselor. Origin: English
- Athelston, From the noble's hill. Origin: English
- Derald, Blend of Daryl and Harold or Gerald. Origin: English, American
- Christine, Christian. Origin: Greek, Latin, American, French, English

- Ellice, Devoted to God. Origin: Greek, Hebrew, English
- Gabriell, God's able-bodied one. Origin: English
- Broc, Badger.Origin: English, Scottish
- Chadwyk, From the warrior's town. Origin: English
- Daisie, Day's eye. A flower name. Origin: English, American
- Alhric, Sacred ruler. Origin: English
- Milford, From the mill's ford. Origin: English, American
- Zayne, or John. Origin: English
- Devyna, From Devonshire. Origin: English
- Brantley, Firebrand. Origin: Teutonic, English
- Blagden, From the dark valley. Origin: English
- Laurie, symbols of honour and victory. Origin: Latin, American, English
- Jady, The gemstone jade; the color green. Origin: English
- Bradleah, From the broad meadow. Origin: English
- Hillary, Joyful, glad. Cheerful. Derived from the Latin name Hilarius. Origin: English, American, Latin

- Christie, 'carrier of Christ, Greek, American, Irish, Scottish, English, Latin
- Burke, Lives in a fortress. Origin: French, English, Teutonic
- Claud, Lame. Origin: English, American, French, Latin, Scottish
- Algar, Noble spearman. Origin: Anglo-Saxon, English
- Clair, Clear. Origin: English, American
- Blondene, Fair-haired; blonde.Spanish Blandina meaning flattering. Origin: English, French
- Christoffer, He who holds Christ in his heart. Origin: English, German, Danish
- Burne, From the brook. Origin: English, Irish
- Christophe, He who holds Christ in his heart. Origin: English, French
- Bryony, The name of a flowering vine used in folk medicine. Origin: Greek, English
- Jenarae, Origin: English
- Ashford, Lives by the ash tree ford. Origin: English
- Cass, Origin: English

- Delavan, Friend; good friend. Origin: English
- Brigg, From the village near a bridge. Origin: English
- Cash, Wealthy man. Origin: English, American, Latin
- Ashlen, Ash trees encircling a pond. Origin: English
- Buster, Origin: English, American
- Kendria, Blend of Ken, meaning royal obligation. Origin: English
- Chapman, Merchant. Origin: Anglo-Saxon, English
- Birkey, From the birch tree island. Origin: English
- Kaitlin, Pure. Origin: Greek, American, Irish
- Gaylene, Joyful. Origin: English
- Brooks, Brook; stream. Origin: English, American
- Bradford, From the broad ford. Origin: English, American
- Dennyson, Dennis' son. Origin: English
- Fylmer, Famed; famous. Origin: English
- Verne, Youthful. Origin: Latin, American, English, French
- Eideard, Rich protector. Origin: Scottish, English, Gaelic

- Del, A masculine or feminine name beginning with Del. Origin: English
- Brickman, Bridge. Origin: English
- Bradley, Origin: English, American
- Celio, Blind. Origin: English
- Oldwina, Special friend. Origin: English
- Bayly, Steward; bailiff. Origin: English
- Ashton, From the town with ash trees. Origin: English, American
- Chelsie, a London district. Origin: English, American
- Fae, Confidence; trust; belief. Origin: English, American, French
- Burns, Son of Byrne. Origin: English
- Aveline, Origin: English, French
- Maryann, Derived from Mary, meaning bitter. Origin: English, American, Hebrew
- Ed, Prosperous protector. Origin: French, American, Biblical, English
- Ashtyn, Town of ash trees. Origin: English, American
- Austine, Origin: English, French, Latin
- Brewer, Brewer. Origin: English
- Ulmarr, Wolf famous. Origin: English
- Salhdene, From the willow valley. Origin: English

- Mardel, Origin: English
- Austen, Origin: English
- Jeramie, in use since the Middle Ages. Origin: English, American
- Farron, Adventurous. Origin: English
- Acton, A town in the U.K. Origin: English
- Osborn, Divine bear. Origin: Norse, Teutonic, English
- Jadira, The gemstone jade; the color green. Origin: English
- Denver, Green valley. Origin: English, American, French
- Carvel, From the villa by the march. Origin: English, French
- Rolfe, Red wolf. Origin: English, Teutonic
- Bentley, clearing covered with coarse grass. Origin: English
- Elwen, Old friend. Origin: English
- Bennett, Right-hand son. Origin: English, American, Latin, French
- Cheryl, Origin: German, American, Welsh, English
- Roddy, Famous ruler. Origin: German, American, English
- Burnette, Bear; brown. Origin: English, Irish
- Oegelsby, Fearsome. Origin: English

- Zane, Gift from God. Origin: Hebrew, American, English
- Grantham, From the great meadow. Origin: English
- Ilde, Battle. Origin: English
- Jillianna, Jove's child.from the masculine Julian. Origin: English
- Daesgesage, Day's eye. Origin: English
- Chess, Camp of the soldiers. Origin: English
- Gala, Singer. Origin: Swedish, English, French, Latin, Spanish, Norse
- Nic, Lord. Origin: English
- Cleantha, Glory. Origin: English
- Cissie, Origin: English
- Chappy, Peddler; merchant. Origin: English
- Caddaham, From the soldier's land. Origin: English
- Davine, Beloved. Feminine of David. Origin: English
- Berke, The birch tree meadow. Also see Barclay and Burke.
- Christian, Christian. Origin: Greek, American, English, Danish, Latin
- Churchill, Lives at the church hill. Origin: English

- Perkins, Son of Perkin. Origin: English
- Dar, Dark. Origin: Gaelic, Hebrew, English
- Kayana, keeper of the keys; pure. Origin: English
- Faer, Traveler. Origin: English
- Barnum, From the baron's home. Origin: English
- Chancellor, Secretary; chancellor. Origin: English
- Aldhelm, Name of a bishop. Origin: Anglo-Saxon, English
- Caroline, Manly. Origin: Scottish, American, French, English, Italian
- Saffron, Origin: English
- Una, Gaelic forms of Agnes. Origin: Gaelic, American, Celtic, Welsh, Irish, English, Latin, Native American
- Braddon, Broad hillside. Origin: English, Irish
- Udayle, From the yew tree valley. Origin: English
- Alexandra, Defender of man. Origin: Hungarian, Italian, Swedish, American, English, Greek
- Marilynn, Blend of Marie or Mary and Lyn. Origin: English, American

- Thornley, From the thorny meadow. Origin: English
- Averel, Fighting boar. Origin: English
- Janicia, Origin: English
- Blisse, Joy. Cheer. Origin: English
- Millman, Mill worker. Origin: English
- Freca, Bold. Origin: English
- Basset, Short. Origin: English, Shakespearean
- Bardulf, Bright wolf, ax-wielding wolf. Origin: English
- Janaya, God has answered. Origin: English
- Jeramy, in use since the Middle Ages. Origin: English, American
- Barbie, Dry. A flower name. Origin: Greek, American, English
- Derby, From Denmark. Origin: Norse, English, Irish, Shakespearean
- Dal, Blind. Origin: Irish, Czech, English, Scottish, Welsh
- Rankin, Little shield. Origin: English
- Aldwine, Wise friend. Origin: English
- Kandi, Modern- ancient hereditary title used by Ethiopian queens. Origin: English, American
- Joanie, Origin: English, Latin, American

- Rangy, From raven's island. Origin: English
- Bartlett, Ploughman. Origin: French, English, Hebrew
- Bancrofft, Pasture; field. Origin: English
- Leonora, Light. Origin: Spanish, American, English, Greek, French, Italian
- Cassy, Origin: English
- Gaby, Woman of God. Origin: French, Italian, English
- Weolingtun, From the wealthy estate. Origin: English
- Beta, meaning either oath of God, or God is satisfaction. Origin: Greek, Hebrew, English
- Alice, noble. Origin: Celtic, American, English, French, German, Shakespearean, Teutonic
- Gyles, Servant. Origin: Gaelic, English
- Danice, Feminine God will judge. Origin: English
- Osbourne, Divine warrior. Origin: English
- Bryan, Brave; Virtuous. Origin: Celtic, American, Arthurian Legend, English
- Zander, Abbreviation of Alexander. Origin: English, American

- Tait, Brings joy. Origin: English, Anglo-Saxon
- Brentyn, Mountain peak. Origin: English
- Gillian, Child of the gods. Origin: English, American, Latin
- Diamond, Jewel name; bridge protector. Origin: English
- Nicki, Abbreviation of Nicole, meaning victory. Origin: English, American
- Herlebeorht, Army strong. Origin: English
- Weorth, From the farm. Origin: English
- Joran, Origin: Scandinavian, English
- Favio, Origin: English, Latin
- Allura, Divine counselor. Origin: English
- Carey, meaning manly. Origin: English, American, Celtic, Irish
- Beomann, Beekeeper. Origin: English
- Birk, Birch tree. Origin: English, French, Scottish
- Aubrie, Rules with elf-wisdom. Origin: English, French, American
- Mercer, Merchant. Origin: English, French
- Radburt, Red haired counselor. Origin: English

- Eddy, Prosperous protector. Origin: English, Greek
- Aegelweard, Noble protector. Origin: English
- Hilde, noble. Origin: German, English, Norse, Teutonic
- Kaelee, meaning: keeper of the keys; pure. Origin: English
- Irvette, Friend of the sea. Origin: English
- Elliott, meaning Jehovah is God. Origin: Greek, American, English
- Nyles, Origin: English
- Atley, From the meadow. Origin: English
- Claybourne, Mortal. Origin: Teutonic, English
- Alfreda, Oracle. Origin: Teutonic, American, English, German, Spanish
- Erwynn, Friend of the sea. Boar-friend. Origin: English
- Radbourne, Lives by the red stream. Origin: English
- Chauncey, Chancellor; secretary; fortune; a gamble. Origin: English, American, Latin, French
- Norwyn, Friend of the north. Origin: English
- Ullok, Wolf sport. Origin: English
- Carmia, Song. Origin: English

- Bennie, Right-hand son. Origin: English, American
- Shelly, From the ledge meadow. Origin: Anglo-Saxon, English, American
- Avelyn, given names Avis and Aveline. Origin: English
- Barrick, Grain farm. Origin: English
- Jayronn, like Jason and Jacob. Origin: English
- Devyn, Divine. Origin: English, French, American
- Eston, From East town. Origin: English
- Brande, Firebrand. Origin: English
- Zeke, Abbreviation of Ezekiel. Origin: English, Hebrew
- Marty, Warrior of Mars. Origin: English, American, Latin
- Haydon, From the hedged in valley. Origin: English, Teutonic, Welsh
- Lisbet, Origin: Danish, English
- Eadmund, Rich benefactress. Origin: English
- Beldane, Lives in the beautiful glen. Origin: English, Teutonic
- Bertrade, Bright counselor. Origin: English

- Chyna, Based on the country name China. Origin: English, American
- Barret, Origin: English, German
- Cassi, Origin: English
- Boot, House. Origin: English
- Brooke, Lives by the stream. Origin: English
- Byford, Lives at the river crossing. Origin: English
- Shepley, From the sheep meadow. Origin: English
- Edee, Spoils of war. Origin: English
- Dalena, Small valley. Abbreviation of Madeline. Origin: English
- Mildryd, Mild of strength. Origin: English
- Bret, A Breton. Origin: Celtic, American, English
- Welton, From the spring farm. Origin: English, American
- Cady, Hillock. Origin: English, Irish
- Deeana, meaning divine. Origin: English
- Derrall, Open. Origin: English, French
- Bron, Origin: African, Anglo-Saxon, English
- Deortun, From the deer park. Origin: English

- Broderick, Surname. Origin: Irish, American, Welsh, Scandinavian, Scottish, English
- Katlynne, Medieval English form of the Irish Caitlin. Pure. Origin: English
- Burnard, Strong as a bear. Origin: English, German
- Clement, Gentle. Origin: English, American, Biblical, Latin
- Quincy, Fifth. Derived from Roman clan name. Origin: English, American, French, Latin
- Hilda, Fighter. Origin: Swedish, American, Anglo-Saxon, Norse, Teutonic, English, German
- Waeringawicum, Fortress. Origin: English
- Beniamino, Right-hand son. Origin: English, Hebrew, Italian
- Bordin, Boar's home. Origin: English
- Hagalean, From the hedged enclosure. Origin: English
- Aubrianne, Rules with elf-wisdom. Origin: English, French
- Cecily, Blind. Origin: Latin, English
- Cinderella, Of the ashes. Origin: French, English
- Barnes, The barns. Origin: English

- Jacey, an abbreviation of Jacinda. Origin: English, American
- Garner, Keeper of grain. Surname. Origin: English, French
- Brently, Hilltop. Origin: Celtic, English
- Christene, Follower of Christ. Origin: English, Latin, American
- Deonna, Divine. Origin: English
- Allayne, Fair; handsome. Also both a (noble, bright) and an abbreviation of names beginning with Al-. Origin: English
- Granger, Farmer. Origin: English
- Radnor, From the red shore. Origin: English
- Waescburne, From the flooding brook. Origin: English
- Bryson, Origin: Scottish, American, English
- Chayce, Huntsman. Origin: English
- Thorndyke, From the thorny dike. Origin: English
- Faerrleah, From the bull's pasture. Origin: English
- Barnaby, meaning son of consolation. Origin: English, Hebrew

- Brionna, The name of a flowering vine used in folk medicine. Origin: English, Greek, American
- Bob, Abbreviation of Robert. Origin: English, American, German
- Rickie, Abbreviation of Richard 'powerful; strong ruler. Origin: English, American
- Kadee, Rhyming, meaning pure. Origin: English
- Joanna, Gift from God. Origin: Hebrew, American, French, Biblical, English, Latin
- Audrey, Strong. Origin: Teutonic, American, Anglo-Saxon, English, Shakespearean
- Cedrina, Modern feminine of Cedric. Origin: English
- Dentin, Valley town. Origin: English
- Radolf, Red wolf. Origin: English
- Dontell, Contemporary phonetic'enduring. Origin: English
- Brittani, Origin: English, American
- Hartman, Strong. Origin: German, English
- PfessSley, From the priest's meadow. Origin: English

- Birkhead, Lives at the birch headland. Origin: English
- Darb, Place where deer graze. Origin: English
- Christeen, Follower of Christ. Origin: English, Latin, American
- Dalen, Rhyming- a historical blacksmith with supernatural powers. Origin: English
- Baird, Bard. Origin: Celtic, Irish, English, Gaelic, Scottish
- Ainsworth, From Ann's estate. Origin: English
- Bankroft, Pasture; field. Origin: English
- Livingston, From Lyfing's town. Origin: English
- Aethelthryth, Wife of King Ecgfrith. Origin: Anglo-Saxon, English
- Deysi, Day's eye. A flower name. Origin: English
- Janaye, meaning 'God has answered. '. Origin: English
- Beretun, From the barley farm. Origin: English
- Chelsy, a London district. Origin: English
- Rodman, Lives by the road 'Guard wisely. Origin: English

- Beornheard, meaning bear-hard. Origin: English
- Roderic, Famous ruler. Origin: English, German, Teutonic
- Ladde, Attendant. Origin: English
- Irwin, Boar friend. Sea friend. Origin: English, American, Anglo-Saxon
- Hartwood, From the stag's forest. Origin: English
- Liza, meaning either oath of God, or God is satisfaction. Origin: Hebrew, American, Hungarian, Greek, English
- Egbert, Name of a king. Origin: Anglo-Saxon, American, English, Teutonic
- Melburn, From the mill stream. Origin: English
- Rangford, From the raven's ford. Origin: English
- Adda, Wealthy. Origin: English, American
- Gael, Joyful. Origin: English
- Welsie, From the west. Origin: English
- Brad, Broad clearing in the wood. Origin: English, American, Welsh
- Elliot, meaning Jehovah is God. Origin: Greek, American, English, French, Scottish
- Gijs, Intelligent. Origin: English

- Marise, Origin: English, Latin, Japanese
- Brandin, Beacon on the hill' or 'gorse-covered hill. Origin: English, American
- Bellden, Beautiful vale/valley. Origin: English
- Kemp, warrior. Origin: English
- Jaye, Swift. Origin: German, English, French
- Buck, Male deer. Origin: English, American, Greek
- Jane, Gift from God. Origin: Hebrew, American, English
- Brienne, Strong. Origin: Celtic, English
- Aswin, Friend with a spear. Origin: English
- Leofric, Dear ruler. Origin: English
- Norton, From the north farm. Origin: Anglo-Saxon, English, American
- Peter, Stone, Origin: English

Chapter 14 – Top 100 Girl Baby Names of 2016

A lot of parents fall into a psychological trap where they disregard a name that they want because of its popularity or unpopularity. I don't want that to happen to you. Therefore, I've listed the top 100 baby names of 2016 for you, but instead of sorting them by popularity – they are sorted from A-Z. I hope you see that I have good intention behind doing this. If you really want to know the top 100 sorted from 1-100, just search on google later. But for now, don't let any of that influence you in regards to choosing the name.

- Aaliyah, Hebrew
- Abigail, Hebrew
- Adalynn, English
- Adeline, English

- Alexa, Greek
- Alexis, Greek
- Alice, German
- Allison, German,
- Alyssa, German
- Amelia, Hebrew
- Anna, Hebrew
- Annabelle, Italian
- Aria, Latin
- Ariana, Welsh
- Arianna, Greek
- Ashley, English
- Athena, Greek
- Aubree, French
- Audrey, German
- Aurora, Latin
- Autumn, Latin
- Ava, Hebrew
- Bella, Latin
- Brianna, Celtic
- Brooklyn, English
- Camila, French
- Caroline, German
- Charlotte, Norse
- Chloe, Greek
- Claire, Latin
- Delilah, Hebrew
- Eleanor, Hebrew

- Elena, Greek
- Eliana, Hebrew
- Elizabeth, Hebrew
- Ella, French
- Ellie, Hebrew
- Emilia, Latin
- Emily, Latin
- Emma, Latin
- Eva, Hebrew
- Evelyn, Celtic
- Faith, English
- Gabriella, Italian
- Gianna, Hebrew
- Grace, Latin
- Hailey, English
- Hannah, Hebrew
- Harper, English
- Hazel, English
- Isabella, Hebrew
- Isabelle, Hebrew
- Jade, Spanish
- Jasmine, Persian
- Julia, Latin
- Katherine, Greek
- Kaylee, Celtic
- Kylie, Celtic
- Layla, Arabic

- Leah, Hebrew
- Liliana, English
- Lillian, Hebrew
- Lily, English
- Lucy, Latin
- Luna, Latin
- Lydia, Greek
- Madeline, Hebrew
- Madelyn, Hebrew
- Madison, English
- Maya, Sanskrit
- Melanie, Greek
- Mia, Latin
- Mila, Slavic
- Naomi, Hebrew
- Natalia, Latin
- Natalie, Latin
- Nevaeh, English
- Nora, Latin
- Olivia, Latin
- Paisley, Gaelic
- Penelope, Greek
- Piper, English
- Ruby, Latin
- Sadie, Hebrew
- Samantha, English
- Sarah, Hebrew
- Savannah, English

- Scarlett, English
- Serenity, Latin
- Skylar, Dutch
- Sofia, Greek
- Sophia, Greek
- Stella Latin
- Trinity, English
- Valentina, Latin
- Victoria, Latin
- Violet, Latin
- Willow, English
- Zoe, Greek
- Zoey, Greek

CHAPTER 15 – TOP 100 BOY BABY NAMES OF 2016

Again, these names are sorted from A-Z and not from 1-100. If you want to know the reason why I did that, just go back to the introduction of the previous chapter.

- Aaron, Hebrew
- Adam, Hebrew
- Adrian, Latin
- Aiden, Celtic
- Alexander, Greek
- Andrew, Greek
- Angel, Greek
- Anthony, English
- Asher, Hebrew
- Austin, Latin
- Ayden, Celtic
- Benjamin, Hebrew
- Bentley, English
- Brandon, English

- Brayden, Celtic
- Bryson, Welsh
- Caleb, Hebrew
- Cameron, Celtic
- Carson, Celtic
- Carter, English
- Charles, German
- Chase, English
- Christian, Latin
- Christopher, Greek
- Colton, English
- Connor, Celtic
- Cooper, English
- Daniel, Hebrew
- David, Hebrew
- Dominic, Latin
- Dylan, Welsh
- Easton, English
- Eli, Hebrew
- Elias, Hebrew
- Elijah, Hebrew
- Ethan, Hebrew
- Evan, Hebrew
- Ezra, Hebrew
- Gabriel, Hebrew
- Gavin, Welsh
- Grayson, English

- Greyson, English
- Henry, German
- Hudson, English
- Hunter, English
- Ian, Hebrew
- Isaac, Hebrew
- Isaiah, Hebrew
- Jace, Greek
- Jack, English
- Jackson, English
- Jacob, Hebrew
- James, Hebrew
- Jason, Greek
- Jaxon, Greek
- Jaxson, English
- Jayden, Hebrew
- Jeremiah, Hebrew
- John, Hebrew
- Jonathan, Hebrew
- Jordan, Hebrew
- Jose, Spanish
- Joseph, Hebrew
- Joshua, Hebrew
- Josiah, Hebrew
- Julian, Latin
- Kayden, Celtic
- Kevin, Celtic
- Landon, English

- Leo, Latin
- Leonardo, German
- Levi, Hebrew
- Liam, German
- Lincoln, English
- Logan, Celtic
- Lucas, Latin
- Luke, Greek
- Mason, French
- Mateo, Hebrew
- Matthew, Hebrew
- Michael, Hebrew
- Nathan, Hebrew
- Nicholas, Greek
- Noah, Hebrew
- Nolan, Celtic
- Oliver, German
- Owen, Welsh
- Parker, French
- Robert, German
- Roman, Latin
- Ryan, Celtic
- Samuel, Hebrew
- Santiago, Latin
- Sebastian, German
- Thomas, Aramaic
- Tyler, English

- William, German
- Wyatt, English
- Xavier, Basque
- Zachary, Hebrew

Conclusion

Hi there! So you've made it all the way to the end. Great job, it shows commitment which is another unique quality that great parents have. I hope that you've enjoyed this book and received a lot of ideas from it. Let's go over what we have covered throughout this book.

In part 1 of this book, you receive some guidance in the form of a step by step process to successfully choosing a name for your baby. You also discovered some mistakes that other parents have done. I believe that knowing that information will allow you to be ahead of 99% of other parents in terms of awareness and protecting your child from unnecessary suffering.

In part 2 and 3 of this book, I introduced you to names with meaning. They were divided into chapters that contained a particular word such as handsome or strong.

In part 4 of this book, you got 3000 more names as well as top lists. I recommend that you now write down a list of 10 potential names that you want for your child. Try to prioritize them and go over chapter 1 and 2 with each name.

Thank you very much for staying with me until the end. I sincerely hope that you've benefited from this book. If you did, can you please leave a review for the book? I would greatly appreciate it, and I will make sure to read it!